2/90

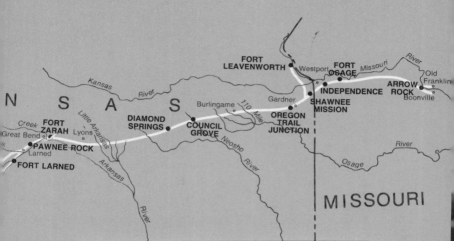

N | S | A | S

Kansas River

Little Arkansas

Creek
FORT ZARAH
Lyons
Great Bend
PAWNEE ROCK
Larned
FORT LARNED

Arkansas River

DIAMOND SPRINGS

Burlingame

COUNCIL GROVE

Neosho River

110 Mile

Gardner

OREGON TRAIL JUNCTION

FORT LEAVENWORTH Westport

SHAWNEE MISSION

FORT OSAGE Missouri

INDEPENDENCE

Old Franklin

ARROW ROCK Boonville

River

Osage River

MISSOURI

Cimarron River

O | K

SAS

IMPRESSIONS

OF THE SANTA FE TRAIL

Other books by the author:

The Old Cathedral
    1965 (2nd edition, 1980)
The Story of Old Ste. Genevieve
    1967 (2nd edition, 1973; 3rd edition,
    1976; 4th edition, 1987).
The Oregon Trail Revisited
    1972 (2nd edition, 1978; 3rd edition,
    1983; 4th edition, 1987.)
History of the Hazelwood School District
    1977
Legacy: The Sverdrup Story
    1978 (2nd printing, 1987)
Leif Sverdrup: Engineer Soldier at His Best
    1980
Maps of the Oregon Trail
    1982 (2nd edition, 1983)
Challenge: The Sverdrup Story Continues
    1988
Images of The Santa Fe Trail
    1988

IMPRESSIONS
O ◇ T H E ◇ S A N T A ◇ F E ◇ T R A I L
A   C O N T E M P O R A R Y   D I A R Y

Gregory M. Franzwa

Foreword by
Nancy Landon Kassebaum

The Patrice Press
St. Louis, Missouri

Library of Congress Cataloging-in-Publication Data

Franzwa, Gregory M.
    Impressions of the Santa Fe Trail.

    Includes index.
    1. Santa Fe Trail—Surveys. 2. Franzwa, Gregory M.—
Diaries. I. Title.
F786.F794   1988   978'.033'09244   88-23869
ISBN 0-935284-62-1
ISBN 0-935284-63-X (pbk.)

Published by
The Patrice Press
1701 South Eighth Street
St. Louis MO 63104

Printed in the United States of America

To Candace
My sister, my friend

CONTENTS

FOREWORD

Nancy Landon Kassebaum
U.S. Senator for Kansas

In 1821 the Santa Fe Trail opened a new trade and migration route between the United States and Mexico. Wagon trains filled with silver and raw materials crossed the land, creating an economic boom for the region between Old Franklin, Missouri, and Santa Fe, New Mexico. Since most of the trail lies in my home state of Kansas and passes through my farm near Council Grove, Kansas, I was pleased to sponsor legislation to declare the Santa Fe Trail a national historic trail.

Impressions of the Santa Fe Trail is Gregory Franzwa's first book on the trail, a day-by-day account of researching the trail as part of the National Park Service study team. In this diary Franzwa relates stories about his travels along the trail and the people he meets—many of whom are descendants of earlier pioneers of the trail.

There is no question that the Santa Fe Trail represents part of our history which should be preserved and commemorated. This book is a very personal rendering by one devoted to just that goal. May I suggest that after reading *Impressions of the Santa Fe Trail,* you consider making your own journey along the trail.

ACKNOWLEDGMENTS

Now having ten books to my credit, I believe I can speak with some authority when I say that works of this nature require a lot of help from a lot of people. In this case, I am especially indebted to my colleagues on this study: Jere Krakow, Ph.D.; Leo Oliva, Ph.D.; Bonita Oliva; Michael Spratt; and John Paige.

Every night, at the conclusion of the day's research, I felt it mandatory to prepare this diary. The work of the day frequently would be so tiring that I couldn't continue past eleven o'clock. I would go to bed and rise at three in the morning to try to finish by assembly time, usually breakfast at 6:30 or 7 A.M.

And why, then, am I indebted to these, my colleagues? Because they had to put up with me in the morning hours, when I was barely functional. I usually would come alive at noon, at which time I could pull my weight out in the field.

Leo, Bonita, Jere, and Marc Simmons also read and commented on this manuscript, shared their knowledge of the trail, and gave me support when I needed it.

But there is one person upon whom I have come to depend, the editor, Betty Burnett, Ph.D. No author worth his salt would attempt to go to press with a book such as this without first submitting it to an editor. Dr. Burnett labored hard to bring light and life to these pages—without taking me out of it, as she said. Whether she succeeded in the readers' judgment will come out later; in my judgment she has done a magnificent job. I am most indebted to her.

—Gregory M. Franzwa
June 30, 1988

INTRODUCTION

When Gregory Franzwa was fourteen years old he was invited to go west on a vacation with his cousin. For a small town Iowa boy the trip was a supreme adventure, one that impressed him deeply. He drank in the sights of the changing countryside and marveled at the magnificent landforms around him.

From that point Franzwa was in love with the geography of the American West. Later he extended his enthusiasm to include geology and Western history. Today he runs a publishing house in St. Louis, Missouri, but his heart is on the prairie and his thoughts are with the westward travelers of the nineteenth century, whether Oregon Trail emigrants, forty-niners, or Santa Fe traders.

The fascination with place led Franzwa to cartography and his acclaimed *Maps of the Oregon Trail.* His plans to do a similar study, *Maps of the Santa Fe Trail,* were stimulated in the spring of 1988 by an offer to join a National Park Service study team, which was surveying the trail in accord with its directive from Congress.

The team, which also included NPS historian Jere

Krakow, Ph.D.; Santa Fe Trail historians Leo Oliva, Ph.D.; and Bonita Oliva, began their adventure on March 15 in Boonville, Missouri. It ended on May 22.

The survey entailed visiting every known site along the trail—locations that had been singled out by nineteenth century travelers as especially significant for one reason or another—and charting the route of the trail, which is still marked in places by the ruts made by hundreds of wagons loaded with trade goods. The team relied heavily on local trail experts, ''buffs,'' to guide them.

From the moment the trip was proposed to Franzwa, he knew he wanted to record his impressions of it and of the people he was to meet. He chose the diary form because he had read and enjoyed hundreds of diaries of nineteenth century travelers.

Of course, twentieth century travel is markedly different from nineteenth. The survey team rode in comfortable automobiles, much of the time on improved roads. The few sections of primitive roads that they bounced over only emphasized the ease of normal travel today.

But today's travelers have experiences that could not have been foreseen a hundred years ago, and these experiences were what Franzwa wanted to record. He is never wholly in the twentieth century, however, and conveys a longing for the romance of the old West. Since that period cannot be recovered, Franzwa hopes that its memory can be preserved through the careful restoration and maintenance of historic sites and through the marking of the trails west that forever changed the face of the nation.

—Betty Burnett
July 15, 1988

IMPRESSIONS

OF THE SANTA FE TRAIL

I. MARCH 15-25, 1988

Tuesday, March 15, 1988

The survey team agreed days ago to meet in the cafe next door to the motel at eight for breakfast. Appropriately, it is named the Santa Fe Restaurant. Jere Krakow from the Denver Service Center of the National Park Service, a Ph.D. historian, will be in charge of our expedition. I had met Jere in Hutchinson during the second symposium of the Santa Fe Trail Association in September. We'd talked often over the last few months, planning the survey, and I felt he was a genuinely nice guy, thoughtful and intelligent and completely committed to the charge that the Congress of the United States has given him to prepare a study of the trail.

With him was Mike Spratt, a recreation planner from the same office, who is in charge of the total study. Tall, lean, young and very bright, Mike has a wry sense of humor

The Comfort Inn and Santa Fe Restaurant, Boonville

that broke the ice at once. Next Leo and Bonita Oliva from Woodston, Kansas, appeared. I had met them in Hutchinson also. Leo is another Ph.D. historian who prefers the outdoors to academia. He left teaching and now farms 2,100 acres. With his gray beard and German high forehead he looks like a Mennonite minister—except he has a book of maps in his hand instead of a Bible. Bonita is almost as sharp as he is, but she doesn't seem to know that.

We were all in good humor. Candidly we assessed each other. This will be a long trip and we'll be together every day. We sipped coffee and discussed strategy. Decisions were made. The others accepted my proposal to make a geographical loop, going to Santa Fe via the Cimarron Cutoff through Oklahoma and circling back to the Arkansas River via the Raton Pass and the Mountain Branch.

I proposed the loop so people wouldn't have to go back to Dodge City to start the second leg. And I wanted to take the Cimarron Cutoff first because the great pilot rocks along

The survey team at the Missouri Intelligencer *marker, from left: Bonita and Leo Oliva, Michael Spratt, Jere Krakow, and Gregory M. Franzwa.*

that road, particularly Wagon Mound, assume the familiar shape going south, but not so clearly coming north. Jere pointed out that our chauvinism makes us forget that Santa Fe, not Missouri, was the starting point for many traders.

We braved a cold wind to look over Boonville. The most important site we saw all day was the road from Old Franklin northwest to the point opposite Arrow Rock. That's the road William Becknell would have used to take his mules to Santa Fe in the fall of 1821. Our guide, H. Denny Davis, publisher of the Fayette *Advertiser,* is positive this is the route. Indeed, the terrain seems to rule out any other way.

We were on that road only a short distance when we stopped at a marker commemorating the pioneer newspaper of Old Franklin, the *Missouri Intelligencer.* Denny feels it is on the site of Broadway, Old Franklin's main street, and shouldn't be moved. But it is on the right-of-way of a proposed bike and hike path and may be shifted to a nearby site.

We followed Highway 87 to a county road, to a few other roads—gravel and dirt—and stopped at a marker denoting Cooper's Fort. There was actual combat here during the War of 1812. Hard to believe, considering how far west it is.

I have just one source for pinpointing the Santa Fe Trail in Missouri, the maps of Hobart Stocking, a professor from Oklahoma who mapped the trail in the 1950s. Here, at least, they were worthless, for they showed a very casual line moving up into the hills. The trail could have been only where we stood, on the site of Highway 87. A bench separates the flood-prone bottomlands from the hills to the right. No way would the land-wise wagoneers or muleteers gone another way—it would have made no sense at all.

At Boonslick we walked down steep paths in densely wooded country and came out into the clear on a bench. Beneath our feet the saline spring issued. I could smell sulfur. Denny urged me to taste it. What the hell, I hadn't been too regular lately anyway, so I dipped my fingers in and tasted them. Yep, they were salty all right, and a little sulfurous too.

There are a number of evaporating kilns in the area, now nearly buried. An upended cast iron salt kettle was beside the path. It gave the place a forlorn look. The salt lick wasn't very successful financially and it was abandoned long ago.

Our next destination was the town of ''just plain'' Franklin, which emerged after a group of dissident New Franklin taxpayers jumped ship. Just at the city limits we

The Boonslick Spring issues between the two posts at left. At far left is H. Denny Davis.

turned into the University of Missouri horticultural station. There we saw the brick home of Thomas Hickman, built in 1821. It had once been a beautiful and spacious place. Now it was a derelict—the roof gaped open and several layers of peeling wallpaper gave it a melancholy air. The ghosts were thick—I could see them in every room.

By now, after our first full day of exploring, we were tired. We were a little different from ordinary tourists because we were keeping careful notes of what we were seeing and attempting to evaluate each site. Is it something the National Park Service should care about? How important is it to the trail? So far we had seen little that was directly related to the trail, but we knew that would change and soon we would be getting more information than we could comfortably absorb. And tomorrow my responsibility for preparing detailed maps would begin in earnest.

Wednesday, March 16, 1988

The morning was crisp and sunny; the wind chill was way down, but that didn't affect our work. We met Roger Slusher in Dover. He and his wife, Donna, are on the faculty at Wentworth Military Academy—he teaches history and social studies and she teaches art. Roger is one of numerous Slushers who have occupied this valley for a century and a half.

He directed us down U.S. 24 toward Lexington. We wanted to reconcile Hobart Stocking's lines with the terrain and with Roger's findings. That, as it turned out, was impossible.

Roger advanced a theory which I had never heard before. We passed perhaps a dozen antebellum homes—most of them beautifully sited on hills—on either side of Highway 24. They obviously had been there since trail days. Wasn't it logical to assume that they faced the Santa Fe Trail? Of course! The trail had to have been the only road around here then. Stocking was away from it by several miles for most of the way. His lines were usually south of ours and through hilly terrain.

We crossed Tabo Creek. It was near here that the original

Slusher settled, as did the first settler, Gideon Rupe. Frankly, the creek didn't look like a formidable obstacle to me, but it must have been a wide, deep river in trail days, for there are many references to a ferry here in nineteenth century documents.

After lunch in Lexington, we walked down the main street of town with Roger, listening to him tell the story of the town. On one corner is the site of the first headquarters of the freighting firm of Russell, Majors, and Waddell. William H. Russell and William B. Waddell had homes in Lexington for a while before they moved to Leavenworth. That same corner served as headquarters for the Confederate general Sterling Price during the Civil War Battle of Lexington.

We walked past the courthouse, where the famous cannonball, fired during that battle, is lodged near the capital of the easternmost column. But it isn't the original. Roger said it had been replaced decades ago, probably because the first one had been spirited away. The hole is still there and that's what counts.

West of Lexington things began to get interesting. I noticed a road snaking along the map just south of Wellington, very close to Highway 24. Stocking's map put the trail less than a mile to the south. I was convinced that we were following the correct route of the Santa Fe Trail and felt for the first time the excitement of discovery. We picked up a gravel road another four or five miles to the west, just south of Napoleon. Here the Stocking line was right on our road. We all agreed: This was the trail.

We were within a few dozen yards of the Jackson County line when the road turned toward the north. About a quarter-mile farther we turned left toward the county line. Seeing nothing in that direction, we returned. As we headed back, retracing our route, Jere noticed a shape on our left, to the north.

"Say," he asked, "isn't that a DAR marker?" He really didn't have to ask because we all knew right away that it was. We turned north and there it was, beautifully sited in the front yard of a well-cared-for farmstead. In the first decade of this century, the Daughters of the American Revolution provided the funds to install hundreds of these granite markers along the Santa Fe Trail. They were positioned with great accuracy.

It was obvious that Stocking was right on the mark here. We went on ahead, discovered an old cemetery, and then retraced the Stocking route to the east. There was no topographical reason why this wouldn't be the Santa Fe Trail. We had confirmation, then, of at least seven miles. Good! Our first real success. And we all agreed with Roger's position that the rest of the trail had to be along the alignment of U.S. 24, all the way back to the Saline County line.

Thursday, March 17, 1988

The weather was stinko. Cold, windy, and spitting sleet. We were determined to stick to our schedule, so off we went. First breakfast at the superintendent's house in Arrow Rock, which was once a stopping place on the trail.

Superintendent Richard Forry and his assistant, Michael Dickey, described the restoration project now going on at the Huston Tavern, a favorite watering hole of SFT traders. Nearly $250,000 was spent restoring the exterior, more than

Michael Dickey

$50,000 on the interior, and they are still working on the second floor.

After the tear-it-down/build-a-new-one mood of the 1950s and 1960s, I am delighted with the current move toward restoration and rehabilitation in America.

After breakfast we visited the Santa Fe Spring, where Becknell stopped on his first mule trip to Santa Fe. It is now covered by a gazebo, and the spring water flows from a pipe in the concrete foundation.

I wanted to photograph the road up to the Arrow Rock landing on the Missouri River. It is on private land which the state wants to acquire. But there isn't any money, said our guides. Richard and Michael dropped no hints about wanting federal help and are in agreement that the state should buy the site.

We certainly can help them convince the state legislature this is important. I have never seen such a diamond in the rough. During the Arrow Rock heyday there were several warehouses on the slope up from the river. Traces of their foundations are still there! As are a multiplicity of ruts, clearly visible, coming up from the landing site. Where there is now a long mudflat, there was then the river, which came to the base of the bluff. Arrow Rock couldn't be Arrow Rock without that landing, and the state should start the pursuit of that site pronto.

We went back up the bluff to see the house that was once the home of George Caleb Bingham. He built it as a two-story home, brick for the first floor and frame for the second. A dogtrot in back connected to a summer kitchen. The well-meaning WPA ''restored'' the house during the depression, tearing off the second floor and converting the building to a single-story structure. They razed the out-buildings. Nothing is believed to be original now but the four brick walls. Inside stands an easel which used to be in one of the artist's Jackson County homes.

Bingham is a genuine Missouri treasure. He painted scenes with a photographer's eye for detail and an artist's feel for composition and color. Some of his paintings, especially *County Election* and *The Jolly Boatmen,* have become American classics, telling a story as rich and expressive as a Mark Twain novel.

The house across the street from the Bingham house is pretty much as it was built in the first half of the nineteenth century. So is the one catercorner. The square to the west is largely vacant, taken by fire many years ago. With that exception, the intersection is a good example of nineteenth century Arrow Rock.

Back at the Huston Tavern Jere hauled out an aerial photo taken of the area by the Department of Agriculture in 1938. He had unearthed it from the National Archives. No one in Arrow Rock knew of its existence, so Jere had made a real find for them. The road up from the landing is clearly evident—it has changed very little from the old days. The photo will be good ammunition for the restorationists when the state does acquire the property down to the landing.

In the midst of the discussion Jean Tyree Hamilton walked in. Boy, do I like her! She and her late husband, Ham, spent most of their lives chasing down the trail in Saline County. Others have told me that I am the most knowledgeable person around on the geography of the Oregon Trail, from Independence to Oregon City. Maybe so, but I have always maintained there isn't a county between here and there where I can't find someone who knows that county a lot better than I do, or ever could know it. Jean Tyree Hamilton is one of those people.

Moreover, when she's asked a question she can't answer, she says she doesn't know. She isn't trying to build any monuments to herself; she just wants what she knows disseminated. Before I left St. Louis I called Jean to see if she had any good lines west of Arrow Rock. Did she ever! She and Ham had mapped the trail all across Saline County, and as we soon learned, they did it with great precision. She sent me a copy of their map, with the rut swales and historic sites marked.

Ginny and Ted Fisher joined us. They are both retired Mizzou professors who now live in Arrow Rock. We headed west out of Arrow Rock in a caravan. Weeks ago I had urged Jere to bring along a couple of CB's or walkie-talkies. He brought two NPS field radios. Leo drew one and Jere kept the other.

We stopped on a gravel road in front of a stone building —Jean had put that on the National Register herself. It was the smokehouse of the old Neff Tavern, a major stop for the freighters on the SFT. Fortunately the sleet was abating a little now, although it was still cold and we had to slog through mud.

At each stop I became more puzzled. I don't know what Stocking was thinking about. His lines were off from one-half to three miles. Ham nailed down the route with rut swales and we have to trust that kind of evidence. Wagons simply wouldn't have gone where Stocking said they did. Not as long as there was an easier way.

After a press conference in Marshall, we drove up to the Greg Riley farm. I could see the locust grove over to the left—a dense copse of trees planted in the trail ruts during the depression. The land, of course, has not been plowed since, thus the ruts are preserved.

As we moved to the west, Jean explained why the wagons were so far north of their presumed road—they were

The caravan at the Neff Tavern site

heading the watercourses which feed into Salt Fork Creek and Rock Creek. The creeks have nasty banks and there was no sense crossing and recrossing if that could be avoided. Stocking recognized this too, and his lines head north just east of Marshall—in the wrong place but at least in the right direction.

We found that the SFT and U.S. 65 were parallel northwest of Marshall. So far the trail has avoided the banks of Salt Fork Creek. Stocking routes the trail under the highway going into Malta Bend, but Ham pegged it a mile north. Ham's lines go under the concrete about two miles east of Grand Pass.

At the Grand Pass cemetery Jean showed us deep swales. Graves had been dug right in the ruts! While our caravan was stopped there, a young woman in a station wagon pulled up to ask what we were up to. Jere told her.

"Wonderful!" she exclaimed. "Glad to hear it. We were all wondering what was going on. I am the mayor and I decided I ought to find out." I presumed that "we" included some of the rest of the seventy-one residents of Grand Pass. We had been there fifteen minutes. Word travels fast in small towns.

Friday, March 18, 1988

After the experience with Stocking's lines in the past few days, I felt uneasy with the lines the Kansas State Historical Society had sent to me. As soon as we were finished with breakfast, I called Bob Knecht in Topeka to see if he could hold the archives open for me Saturday afternoon, so I could transfer lines directly from the 1855-57 cadastral plats. No way. But he said the library would be open from 8 A.M. to noon. I decided to go then, even though it would mean leaving at an indecent hour.

Our first appointment of the morning was with Pauline Fowler. Polly provided me with an abundance of help when I was writing *The Oregon Trail Revisited* and I feel a deep camaraderie with her. Jere, the Olivas, Polly, and I spent at least an hour comparing notes. I took the line she had, drawn by William Clark, west from Fort Osage and put it on the present county map. (Clark established Fort Osage in 1808 and by the mid-1820s it was the westernmost rendezvous point for SFT traders.) Polly feels this is the best line by far for the SFT in this area. Stocking's line is an average of one mile south.

We took off for Fort Osage, which was still closed for the

Fort Osage

winter. We looked at the so-called trail on the north edge
of the cemetery. I don't believe it is the trail at all. Perhaps
the trace marks a road that once came up from George
Sibley's house, which was down on the bottom somewhere.
Up on the flat it is just that—as flat as if it had been graded.
I'd bet it was.

We drove to the west several miles, poked around and
found the most likely spot for the crossing of the Little
Blue—great site, I think. And very logical. Then we moved
down the line and up a narrow lane to the site of the Blue
Mill, once operated by James and Robert Aull, the Lexington merchants. Nothing is left but a few courses of foundation stones stuck in the bank of the Blue River. There
is a two-car garage across the lane made of the same stone,
presumably from other portions of the foundations of the
mill. The superstructure of the Blue Mill, according to Polly,
was made of walnut logs and was three stories high.

We went as far as we could go toward the Blue Mills
Landing on the Missouri River—a few dozen yards short

of the bluff. A locked gate stopped us. No matter. We know where the landing is and maybe someday it will be opened to the public.

The drive to the upper landing at Wayne City was a joy for me. On an insufferably hot August day in 1983, during the first convention of the Oregon-California Trails Association, a marker had been dedicated there. Vandals wrecked it only a few weeks later. It was replaced right away, but to prevent a recurrence, Missouri Portland Cement Co., which owns the site, built a guardhouse at the gate and barred admission. The brush, which had been so neatly cut for the ceremony in 1983, grew back and once again obscured the view of the river and the landing.

Now, not only has the marker been replaced, the gate was open and the guardhouse gone. Furthermore, the brush was cut and the view of the river below was magnificent. God bless Jane Mallinson—I know she must be the one who had accomplished that little miracle.

We drove to Independence Square, where some of the trains assembled, and then over the Independence-Westport Road. It is difficult to get a sense of western history in this densely crowded urban area. Lines of cars backed up at red lights, Amoco stations and Pizza Huts, half-deaf kids with ghetto blasters, and old folks in jogging suits make it all but impossible to see the lines of wagons that once headed west from here. Of course life in Independence was just as crowded, hectic, and noisy then as it is now, but we who are seeking history find irritation in today's traffic and romance in yesterday's.

Sylvia Mooney has tried for years to establish Cave Springs as a trail campsite but so far no one has found a reference to it in trail documents, even though it would have been a day's ride from Fort Osage and a logical stopping place. She feels that it was too important a spring not to have been a campground for emigrants, traders, or others moving west. I think she is right but my opinion is not a primary source.

After we toured her Cave Springs area, Sylvia escorted us to several other places, including Aunt Sophie's Cabin on Blue Ridge Boulevard, which I entered for the first time. It is in bad shape. Aunt Sophie was a slave of the Rice family and lived in that cabin from trail days until well into this century. The Rice-Tremonti estate is for sale; I hope it is acquired by responsible people, as the old trailside farm is a historic site of some consequence.

Sylvia took us to two sites where there were supposed to be ruts. One was in back of a nearby residence. No ruts that we could see. The other was in a Wild West promoter's lot. We slithered through mud to where they were alleged to be. Jere found something resembling ruts, but almost certainly they are not trail related, for they are down in a draw and we know the wagons followed the Blue Ridge. More baloney. Sylvia should have seen through this.

We cut over to 103rd Street to show Jere the site of the Watts Mill. Kansas Citians are now trying to raise the money to replace the old mill. Why didn't they think of its value in the 1950s when they destroyed the original? No one was thinking of preservation then, that's why.

A superb piece of historic restoration, which shows what determination can do, is the Alexander Majors House. The elderly owner, who lived there alone, left the property in trust to a close friend, Terry Chapman. Terry, an architect, has worked like a horse fixing the place up. The Russell, Majors, and Waddell National Historic Association deserves commendation, too.

We took Sylvia home and on the way passed through Swope Park. Polly observed that this was the route of a second Santa Fe Trail. Jere feels we ought to include it in the survey. I'm not convinced, and look forward to seeing the documentation.

At old Westport I showed the Olivas Tom Beard's sculpture in Pioneer Park of Majors, John Calvin McCoy, and Jim Bridger. It is a powerful work, and I am mighty proud of my membership in the Westport Historical Society, that amazing little outfit who fought for this memorial and won. Another group wanted a memorial to artist Thomas Hart Benton, who lived in Westport. As much as I admire Benton's work, I feel that Westport belongs to the pioneers.

The historical society had help from the Native Sons of Kansas City. Larry Phister, who led the fight, died just a few months short of the dedication. I gave a short talk at that affair last October. It was an unseasonably cold, windy day, but the turnout was large and the mood jubilant. Everywhere was the satisfied feeling of accomplishment.

The Olivas and I had dinner at Stanford & Sons. They had been there before and wanted to go back. They were not so much enthralled by the Jim Bridger connection as they were by the strawberry cheesecake.

My thoughts went back to my old friend Bill Goff, who died just a few days before Christmas 1987. Bill told me that the Stanford & Sons building had replaced one old Jim Bridger had owned on that site. When the restaurant people bought it and began remodeling it, Bill watched, his amazement growing daily. This was no replacement—this was the original! He contacted me in time to change the type before *The Oregon Trail Revisited* went to press, bless him. He was another one who didn't know how to say no to anyone who asked for help for historic preservation projects. We miss Bill Goff.

Saturday, March 19, 1988

Five-thirty came mighty early. After breakfast I took off for Topeka, pulling up in front of the Kansas State Historical Society at one minute after eight. Bob Knecht was already at work, and he helped me get started with the cadastral plats. It has been twenty years since I had worked with them and I was a bit rusty. There are more than thirty Kansas counties to decipher. I got half-done before the bell rang and the building closed.

I had mixed emotions about what I found. First, the half-size maps sent to me by KSHS with the trails marked were very rough. The trail lines scaled out to be several hundred feet wide. Second, I found some very substantial variances of transcription. Well, that's why I was checking up on them. I am satisfied now. I'll be back in a week to finish up.

I headed west. I wanted to see the new museum building of the KSHS, a few miles west of town. I have been a member of the Society for years, but I seldom get to Topeka. The new museum is just as impressive as people say it is, from the statue of the white buffalo in a reflecting pool outside the main building, to a pusher biplane (similar to the Wright Flyer), which was built and flown in Kansas in the second decade of this century. With a few artifacts, some memorabilia, photographs, lights and shadows, that bittersweet wonderment (''where oh where has time gone?'') is almost enveloping.

Sunday, March 20, 1988

A day off! Yippie! And the first day of spring! Double Yippie!

It was time to go to work on the maps, marking the trail with a red line. Absorbed in my work, I realized with a start, hey, this is fun!

Monday, March 21, 1988

A day at Leavenworth. The leader of our tour was Stephen J. Allie, the museum curator. He showed us a great overland freight wagon, which I photographed broadside. I am going to have a photographic studio blow that up so Lisa can trace out a logo. I know this one is legit because Steve said the iron was found down near Corral Creek, the headquarters for the Russell, Majors, and Waddell freighting operation for the army.

After we toured the buildings, we headed down from the overlook toward the bottomlands. There we saw the foundations for the warehouse. Again, as at Arrow Rock, the river was blocks away. At one time it scoured up against this bank. Looking up from the warehouse we could see a deep cut, excavated by the freighters. It must have been used to haul their wagons up to the bench upon which Fort Leavenworth was built. The cut is a block long, with

Warehouse foundations at Fort Leavenworth

OT/SFT markers at either end. Terrific!

Steve then directed us toward the main parade, explaining that claims that the old stone wall was built for protection against the Indians were untrue. A photograph was recently found proving that it wasn't built until 1872, after Indians had disappeared from the area.

The main powder magazine was smack in the middle of the parade and designed so that if it were to blow, it would blow straight up. I suppose that would save lives.

Layers of history engulf the fort. It was established in 1827 by Col. Henry Leavenworth and hasn't stopped growing since. The "Rookery," built in 1832, had been in existence almost 100 years when young Douglas MacArthur received engineering training there. As we passed the disciplinary barracks, I wondered how much frustration and anger had been billeted behind those walls. A statue of Ulysses S. Grant evokes thoughts of the Civil War and the cemetery holds the graves of soldiers killed at Little Big Horn. (The grave of William Sloan, brother of Marion Sloan Russell, is in the city's cemetery. Russell's autobiography, *Land of Enchantment,* is a beautiful description of life on the Santa Fe Trail and one I frequently consult.)

Judging Fort Leavenworth as a significant trail site was easy. In the spring of 1846 a border skirmish between Mexico and the U.S. escalated into war. Volunteers poured into Fort Leavenworth to sign up with Col. Stephen Watts Kearny's Army of the West. In mid-June the First Missouri, commanded by Alexander Doniphan, left the fort in pursuit of Mexicans along the Santa Fe Trail. A week or so later Kearny led his troops on their historic trek toward the annexation of New Mexico and the conquest of California. The Mormon Battalion, fired by Brigham Young's vision of a heavenly "manifest destiny," followed in mid-August.

Then, the slope toward Corral Creek was alive with oxen—as many as 8,000 head. Russell, Majors, and Waddell kept 1,000 freight wagons shuttling between the fort and Santa Fe to supply the Army of the West. The entire valley would have been filled with oxen, wagons, men, and supplies. What a sight that would have been!

After lunch we drove down Highway 7 and then over to Highway 32 a few miles, to Grinter's Ferry. The great steamboat gothic house still commands a view over the river. We went up to tour the place. It was closed on Mondays.

Earlier caravans reached the SFT by proceeding southeast along the old road to Fort Scott and joining the main trail just west of New Santa Fe. To do that they had to cross the Kaw.

Steve said the trail came down about over the present road and crossed the river dead ahead. If so, how did the wagons get there? We went up the hill and turned onto Swartz Road. We hadn't gone a quarter mile when I looked over to the right and saw ruts heading right for the Grinter house. We went back another block on that alignment and saw nothing. Another tier back. Still nothing. We knocked on doors, hoping to find someone who knew where more ruts were. No answer.

We went back to Kansas City to the Seth Ward and William Bent homes. Ward is best known for being a sutler on the Oregon Trail, but he did travel the Santa Fe Trail as well. Bent was a founder of the famous Bent's Fort in Colorado. When we reached the houses, which are on the same lot, the sun was just right for taking pictures.

Next we considered Shawnee Mission, the former training school for Indian children. Was it an important trail site? I didn't think so, but Jere felt we should at least visit it. So we did. There, imbedded in a big old tree, Bonita found an old porcelain-enameled SFT sign. Marc Simmons mentions these in his *Following the Santa Fe Trail*.

None of the team had seen Westport Landing, so I drove us through that concrete maze that had so bedeviled me two decades ago and finally got onto the levee at the boat landing. Parking where we shouldn't, we walked where we shouldn't, right down to the riverboat. I approached the young guy on the boat, who asked, "Are you guys officials or something?''

We told him we were with the National Park Service doing a survey of the Santa Fe Trail and added that the results ought to bring him some extra business in a few months. He smiled and eagerly waved us aboard.

I showed the troops the limestone benches which led up to the bluff, but instead of listening to my lecture, they became fascinated with the train coming down over the A.S.B. lift bridge. Both Leo and Jere were grinding away with their video cameras as it thundered over us.

When I finally got their attention, I explained that the well-known *United States Illustrated* engraving of the area was wrong, because it shows a curve in the bank which isn't there and never could have been. And that artist William H. Jackson painted a myth—a flat levee with no limestone bluff. I wonder if the old guy had ever seen the place.

Tuesday, March 22, 1988

Sometime during the night we were joined by Les Vilda of Nebraska. Les is a modern-day mountain man. Totally unshorn, his black beard hangs to his chest. His raiment, from his feather-bedecked hat to his stained buckskin ''possible sack'' is authentic. Les is a soft-spoken enthusiast of the Santa Fe Trail. At the Hutchinson convention he was named ''Santa Fe Trail Ambassador,'' because of the goodwill he engenders during his travels. He has walked the trail twice with his burro, Joker.

We found the Mahaffie House to be a beautiful two-story cut stone structure. Curiously, the cornerstone is almost at the top of the building—1865. Michael Duncan is laboring to bring the house back to the way it was when it was a stage station—one of the best two on the line it has been said, and a convenient lunch stop after leaving Westport. He gave us an enthusiastic tour through the house, pointing out the additions, then offered to take us around Olathe, first to the square where there is an impressive marker on the corner.

My reaction was ho hum. Markers may be impressive if you are looking at just one or two, but after so many, they get tiresome. Those which mark the trail serve a noble purpose, even if they do put me to sleep. They remind folks of what happened here. I daresay that ninety percent of the home folks would never have heard of the SFT were it not for these markers. Another factor that keeps the trail in people's minds is the plethora of businesses which use SFT as part of their name. Right across Santa Fe Trail Street from our motel is the Santa Fe Trail Body Shop, for instance.

South of town is the Lone Elm Campground. Somebody has set the DAR marker there on a new concrete base. Good for them. The last time I saw it—probably a dozen years ago—the bottom half was underground.

With Michael leading the way, we cut across Don Willsey's land to about the center of the section. There we saw the spring. Some spring! In a copse of trees is what appears to be an overgrown cistern, rimmed in concrete blocks and topped with used railroad ties. No water bubbles out—or even trickles.

We went west. Leo continued on to Baldwin City to pick up Katharine B. Kelley. After lunch we drove to the place south of Gardner where the Oregon Trail split from the Santa Fe. We assembled at the big state marker in the triangle formed by the intersection of Highway 56 with a gravel road. After the others admired the marker, they piled back in the cars and started to move on.

Hey, what the hell! You can't do that! I stopped them, hollering, "Don't you want to see where the trail really split?" They must have thought they were already there. So I led a surprised group up the gravel road to the half-section line, turned into the field beyond the fence and followed north through the dirt along it for a quarter mile. Thick black dust billowed around us, kicked along by a Kansas wind that was a first cousin to a tornado. I stopped, but kept the car door closed until all four cars had stopped moving, because the dust from the other three was blowing right up my tailpipe.

When we were all out of the car, I directed them to the barbed wire fence and pointed east. "This is the place," I said as Brigham-like as I could. Les volunteered the information that the farmer who put in the little reservoir had uncovered tons of wagon iron when he built the dam.

Our next stop was the Black Jack ruts, a couple of miles east of Baldwin City. Three tremendous swales run through the pasture. The thatch had been burned off and they were clearly visible. I had had a terrible time finding them last fall, when the grass was waist-high.

Katharine says the fellow who owned the land, Russell Hay, deliberately left it in pasture because he didn't want to destroy the swales. At some point he found a couple of large rocks and apparently carved them himself, claiming that they were Sibley markers. They are as phoney as Father Padilla's graves! I guess some people admire history so much they want to fabricate it themselves.

This swale in Black Jack Park turns into the woods, toward the spring.

Amelia Betts spent hours repainting the lettering on DAR markers.

One of the swales we were following turns into Black Jack park, where there is a small spring, and the others head over to the former town of Palmyra. We did too. Katharine led us to the "Santa Fe Spring," the only remnant of the long-disappeared town of Palmyra. Blacksmiths and others set up shop here at one time to earn a living from the freighters. A well was dug for them to lure them to town.

Katharine took us to her modest bungalow next. She and her friend, Amelia J. Betts, lived there for more than fifty years. Both graduated from Baker University in 1932. Katharine took a degree in botany and Amelia, who died recently, had one in journalism.

These two women created, paid for, and installed nine historic markers throughout Douglas County. Someone told me the cost was right at $900 each. I don't know, maybe they could afford it, but my guess is that the expense hurt. They did it anyway, out of love for the Santa Fe Trail and their home county. Life would be pretty bare without people like Katharine and Amelia.

Katharine's enthusiasm now is bird banding. "Banded over 1,100 birds since January," she said. She catches them in traps, clamps a tiny aluminum band around their legs, and turns them loose. Her birds have been sighted from northwestern Canada to the coast of Maine.

We went out in search of the markers, first to Trail Park, north of town, where the SFT proceeds northwesterly right under the road. A mile away we were forced into an east-west alignment. We continued west about a tenth of a mile and saw them: big swales! Oh, those suckers are deep! Standing in them I could see that they align perfectly with the gravel road leading from Trail Park.

We went on to Brooklyn, where Quantrill and his infamous raiders burned everything but the saloon. To Globe, a town now gone. To Willow Springs, now largely inaccessible. To Flag Springs.

Katharine said the DAR was wrong here, Flag Springs wasn't here at all, but in the next county west, a mile west of Overbrook. When she found this out she wrote to Marc Simmons to tell him that she and Amelia had misled him earlier. That's what trail folks do, share information and try to help each other out.

Katharine had made arrangements with a fellow named Featherstone to meet us at Simmons Point, where there are ruts and a stage station just behind the relay tower. We drove in. No Mr. Featherstone, but here is one sensational ruin of a stage station! It had been lived in not too many years ago, but now the windows are gone and the building is ramshackle. Featherstone is perplexed, according to Katharine. He would like to "do something" with the property, but what? Good question. To restore the stage station would take a bundle.

We went on to the Osage fishing lake where there were good ruts on the east side of the access road. Katharine was good for one more site. "Would you like to stay with us until we find the Harris-Magee Stage Station?" I asked her. Foolish question.

"I'm game," she said with a grin.

Following directions in the Simmons book, we turned hard around a marker and then onto a monster of a dirt road. Reminded me of South Pass. Okay, I told myself, keep the left suspension on the shoulder, right suspension on the crown. Cross over at a sharp angle when necessary. We bounced down .2 mile of that when we came onto a grassy, park-like clearing. There, in the middle was a spectacular ruin. It was gorgeous. Half the stones are on the ground now, but many beams are still in their pockets. We went in gingerly. Dangerous stuff. One good sneeze and the whole works might cave in on us.

I spotted Les moving over toward a smaller building to the north. That was half stone too, and also falling down. We walked through. Traces of plaster were on some of the walls; one even had the pattern of wallpaper still on it.

Out in back was a large mound with a fair-sized opening. A fruit cellar. It was a frightful-looking place. "Les," I said, "I'll bet there is one last jar of blackberry preserves down there with your name on it."

Council Grove's famous Last Chance Store

"Yeah, well, I'll bet there is a rattler down there with my name on it. I'm staying up here."

The wind was down now. Jere and Leo went east to take Katharine home. Alone I headed south on 75 to hit a little road that would take me over to Osage City and 56. The sun sank hot and orange and clear; the light seemed to have a peculiar staying quality to it. I was some twenty miles east of Council Grove when it really started to get dark, and sleep wanted to come. No way. Go away, sleep. About ten miles out I could see the blinking top light of a radio tower. Then I crested a hill and saw a necklace of white pinpoints of light laying on the horizon. Would I get to the famous Hays House before it closed? Before I fell asleep

Kansas's Madonna of the Trail *stands in a Council Grove park.*

and ended up in the ditch? 7:24 was my guess. I was off a minute. I ordered the stuffed pork chop special. It was perfect.

Later, as I looked out the window of the Cottage House at the streetlight glinting off the car, I could hear the distant whistle of a train nearing Council Grove. A branch of the Santa Fe, perhaps, the very line which did the trail in. It is a beautiful sound that takes me back to my boyhood in Glidden, Iowa, when the trains loaded with tanks and other instruments of war roared through that little town on the Great Plains. Their only acknowledgment that we existed was a mournful whistle, dopplered down a couple of tones as it sped past the elevator. My Mama Done Tole Me, Son, About the Blues in the Night. They're here.

Wednesday, March 23, 1988

The leaders of Council Grove seem to be intelligent and quite aware of their heritage. I wish they would all get together and purge themselves of their silly slogan, ''Birthplace of the Santa Fe Trail.'' That is baloney. That title belongs to Old Franklin. ''Start of the Santa Fe Trail'' also belongs there, or Arrow Rock, or even Independence or Westport, but surely not Council Grove. They've based their claim on the fact that many of the trains organized here; certainly that doesn't qualify them as the ''birthplace.'' They have so much legitimate stuff here. They don't need the baloney.

Donald Cress also joined us. He's an insurance agent and owns the old bank building across Main Street from the Conn Store as well as a ranch. A slim, wiry six-footer, he is to be our guide for the day. Donald knows the trail in this vicinity very well; he has researched it carefully and has ridden it horseback several times. In fact, he is presently organizing a trail ride from Four Corners through Council Grove and on to McPherson. He expects to have from forty-five to sixty riders.

Between Donald and Les Vilda we are well guided. What one doesn't know the other does. We headed into Burlingame, to the newspaper office. It doesn't have the name of the paper on the building, only the word "Newspaper." Maybe that's its name, the Burlingame *Newspaper*.

As we drove out of town, I looked to the left as the car in front of me slowed down. The sight was staggering— the ruins of the old Havana Stage Station, just 150 yards from the highway. I parked and walked over the plowed but unplanted ground. It is gorgeous, almost as stark as the Harris-Magee station we saw last night. How come these things aren't on the Oregon Trail?

Somehow the others liked my driving and wanted me in the lead. Donald drives a 4x4 pickup, and I thought he should go first. Last night I was the one up front slithering on the way to the Harris-McGee stage station. Here I was in front again on the way to the Dragoon Creek crossing.

I had put on a new set of Michelins before I left St. Louis. Good thing. The traction was terrific. Even when I'm going three to five miles an hour, some quick decisions have to be made on crossing over from one shoulder to the other, always on a fairly sharp diagonal. Better to have one wheel in trouble than two. I came to the end of the rutted dirt road. We could have gone left into a farmyard, or right, down a cliff to the crossing, which I could see down below.

Dragoon Creek Crossing

I stopped. They stopped. We walked down. I suppose some-one could drive down to the crossing—in a Sherman tank.

There's a flat rock bed to the creek, which extends several yards out of the water to the cliff. It's as slick a crossing as I have ever seen. But no wheel grooves. Donald says that is because the rock flakes off, and proceeded to kick away some of the top layer. Well, what the heck, does it grow back? Doesn't make sense to me, but they had to cross somewhere and this seems to be an ideal place. I could see where someone had been coming down this way from the other side.

Leo demonstrated his watertight shoes—air can get out but water can't get in—and walked across on the ford. Never more than two or three inches deep. We all hunkered back up the hill. Bottles and papers littered the place. At the top of this otherwise sylvan setting was a monster trash heap. Somehow we all got turned around and I ended up leading the way back out again.

A big black tank on stilts, probably full of road oil, was on the right. We turned into a paved area behind it which once was the old highway. Right beside it was a lone grave surrounded by a pipe fence. Sam Hunt, the dragoon for whom the creek was named. He died there in 1835.

We turned left at the next corner, looking for the crossing of Soldier Creek. I wanted to keep moving, but Jere wanted to search it out. He's right; I'm wrong. No sign down on this dirt road, but up ahead an elderly couple was planting potatoes in their front yard. Les and Jere decided to drive on ahead and ask them if they knew about the crossing. We stayed behind in the car. About ten minutes later they all came back, the farmer driving his pickup, his wife beside him, Les and Jere behind.

They led us a quarter-mile back toward the highway, opened a wire gate in the fence, and drove into the field. They headed west down the fencerow as far as they could go and we all got out. There I met Clayton and Thelma Shepherd. Clayton is tall, friendly, and easygoing. Thelma is short, round, and gasping for breath, as if in a state of perpetual excitement. He is seventy-nine, she seems to be a few years short of that. They are genuinely glad to help.

Mostly, they're overjoyed to see Les Vilda again. They remembered his first time through, in 1984, when he was accompanied by another guy and two very well-built young women. Last year he came through alone, with his donkey. And every place we've gone, everyone we met was delighted to see Les again, without exception. The mayor and the Chamber of Commerce of Council Grove. Donald Cress. Whenever we knocked on a door to seek help, whoever answered remembered Les with fondness.

Thelma and Clayton Shephard, left, at the crossing of Soldiers Creek. At right are Donald Cress and Les Vilda.

I found this surprising because of his looks. His mountain man image is a lot like the hippie look of the 1960s. His hair is very long. Rural people are not known for their tolerance of guys who look like he does.

But Les exudes kindness and tolerance. He told me that folks are suspicious and standoffish when they first meet him, but they warm up quickly, when they see he is clean, doesn't smell bad, and doesn't smoke funny cigarettes. He is, in fact, one delightful young man. He carries a notebook with him; in it are the names of the people he has met. And of the hundreds of people listed in it, I doubt if there's one who thinks unkindly of Les.

Clayton and Thelma took us right to the ford. We looked back to the northeast, to the black tank on the horizon, and sure enough, the ruts were headed right for us.

I think Clayton and Thelma would like to have invited us all to dinner that noon; probably roast beef and mashed potatoes, but we said good-bye, expressing our thanks.

On to the town of Wilmington. Nothing is left there but a little rock schoolhouse. At this point we started seeing large wagon-wheel markers, put up by the Burlingame Boy Scout troop as part of their hiking trail to Council Grove. Well, at least some kids will learn history.

To the Chicken Creek crossing. This time Donald, Jere, and the rest were in front. I stopped before the crossing, watching them on the bridge. Suddenly a woman was at my window. "You folks looking for something?"

"Yep. The Santa Fe Trail."

"Right here. You got the right place. Right there is where a wagon turned over and a guy drownded. The crippled guy got ahold of his horse and saved his life but the other guy died."

This was Ruby Hedman. Slender, dark-complexioned, in her sixties, I supposed. She continued, her enthusiasm building, "That depression up there is where my house was. Burned to the ground. I lost my husband last year and live here alone. Folks come by ever once in awhile looking for the Santa Fe Trail. Say, isn't that the guy with the donkey up there?"

I introduced her to the others, who came back to my car. She told us of the exploits of Jesse James in the area. Jesse must have been at least sixty people to have done all he is given credit for.

Donald knew of some rocks grooved by wagon wheels near the Diamond Creek Ranch. We stopped on the gravel road, climbed though the barbed wire fence and over the knoll. We found some rut depressions here but no rocks. Donald couldn't find them either. We fanned out. I could remember seeing rocks like that in Carson Pass, in California. I poked around a wild plum bush and managed to find a few rocks which obviously had been scarred and fractured by wagon wheels.

The Diamond Spring was the next stop. I was very disappointed last October when I first saw this spring surging up in a concrete stock tank. Somehow springs don't seem pristine when they come up inside concrete.

Well, turns out I didn't have the spring at all. It is up a gully about fifteen feet away. Instead of surging up inside a concrete tank, it flows out a plastic drainpipe. The tank received some of the outfall. While we were gawking, the ranch manager, Jerry O'Conner, rode up on a handsome horse. Several other ranch hands, also mounted, followed. He talked, we listened, and then we left, heading for Council Grove.

But first someone wanted to see Father Padilla's monument. At the base we climbed in the back of Donald's pickup, and lurched up the steep hill to the rock obelisk, which was dedicated to Coronado's priest, who accompanied the expedition to Quivira. He returned to this area for some serious converting, and the native Muricans turned him into a pincushion with their arrows.

The view from the monument was marvelous. The sun was dropping rapidly, catching the tops of the Council Grove buildings in its last orange rays. At last we headed for Hays House and dinner.

Thursday, March 24, 1988

This was supposed to be a short day. Jere planned to split for Wichita at about noon to catch a plane for Denver. We drove to the bridge over Mile-and-a-half Creek (the mileage was measured from the Diamond Spring). The crossing is nearby, probably right where we were. We continued on to the crossing of Six-mile Creek and turned into a ranch driveway at a DAR marker.

Raleigh Sill and his wife, Bonnie, were waiting for us. Raleigh gave us a quick talk about the stone ruin a few feet away from him—he was born in an upstairs room there more than seventy years ago. Then he turned the show over to Bonnie. She is a retired English teacher and launched into a terrific dissertation on the history of the place. The Indian attacks, the tough times of the settlers, the days as a stage station, the glory years.

Then we piled in Raleigh's pickup and moved out of the barnyard to the several deep rut swales in a nearby field. We crossed the dry Six-mile Creek. Raleigh pointed out a meander of the stream bed, where he says there is a rock bottom, and the logical place for a crossing. We never would have found that without his help.

We stayed too long there, but decided to press on to Lost Spring anyway. I was running on fumes, so I pulled into the only gas station in town. No credit cards here; but the owner takes cash.

Les was in the back seat. "Hey-y-y, you're back!" That

The ford of Six-mile Creek

was Joe Alvarez, station owner, speaking to Les.

West of town we came to Lost Spring. Donald knows the rancher very well. He was fixing up some fences, getting ready for Donald's trail ride. "Hey-y-y, you're back!" That was big Fred Shields, owner of the Lost Spring property, greeting not Donald, but Les Vilda.

The time evaporated. The troops were ready to cut down to the little town of Durham and have lunch. Jere wanted to make one more site before leaving for Wichita. We managed to do both.

In Durham we drove by the little cafe where Joan Myers had taken a shot published in her photo book of the SFT. Les said there was a better place farther down the line. A couple of blocks later and we're there. We walked in the door of Meier's Food and Fuel and to our right, at one of the four tables, were three elderly people.

"Hey-y-y, you're back! We got your pitcher right here on the wall. Come look at it!" Sure enough, there was a color print of Les and his donkey, taken last year. This guy is a celebrity.

We pressed on to the Cottonwood Crossing. It is on the property of a Mennonite rancher, Claude Unruh, who was out in front of the house. We stopped. "Hey-y-y, you're back!" Guess who he was talking to.

I was itching to get to Topeka to get some research done before the historical society closed and I arrived at 4:15, just fifteen minutes before the DOT closed. This is where I found the cadastral plats from the 1855 U.S. Survey in 1971, thus unlocking the Kansas mystery as to the precise route of the Oregon trail.

Right now I needed county maps to bring the Fort Leavenworth road down to the Santa Fe Trail. I made it to the right desk just in time, but the microfilms of the cadastrals are now at the historical society and there's no way I could get there before five. I'd have to wait until tomorrow.

Friday, March 25, 1988

I busted my tail getting to the society by eight, only to find it opens at nine on weekdays. I checked out the microfilm reels and traced the old roads down to Topeka, then worked on the last half of Kansas. Panic! I ran out of 1856 surveys at Dodge City. Bob Knecht tried to help by providing the Brown survey of 1827. No good. North is at the bottom instead of at the top and there are no coordinates. I chose to go nuts my own way and did not try to figure that guy out.

It was a crusher of a job, but I found the right lines again the next county over. It was nearly four o'clock when I finished. Dinner and a gallon or so of black coffee and I was ready for the long grind into St. Louis.

II. APRIL 3-12, 1988

Easter Sunday, April 3, 1988

The base maps for the Kansas part of *Maps of the Santa Fe Trail* are all laid out now. The biggest problem I faced was the lack of specific information on the road from Fort Leavenworth south to an intersection of the trail. There are some primary lines—the Fort Scott military road crosses at Grinter's Ferry and proceeds south down the state line to intersect the Santa Fe Trail just west of New Santa Fe. Another intersects the road from Westport southwest of Olathe. We showed that too. Another, the Fort Riley military road, comes west to the Topeka area and evidently crosses the Kaw where the Papin Ferry was and intersects the SFT at the Narrows, near Baldwin City.

Showing all the routes makes an awful hodgepodge of maps. There may be still another line. Bill Chalfant has platted one from a series of known points and the network of Indian trails which connected them.

Lisa Taylor worked all day Saturday with me at the press. She tackled the map boards and the overlays with the good cheer which characterizes her personality. It was a confusing situation even to an old goat like me, who went through it with *Maps of the Oregon Trail* and *Trail of the First Wagons over the Sierra Nevada*—it could be terribly confusing to a youngster who had never done it before.

It was a good way to spend Easter Sunday, heading west in a heavily-laden Chrysler that's in perfect condition, with the morning sun to our backs and the anticipation of tracing the Santa Fe Trail in front of us.

South toward Newton, Kansas, just past a grove of trees we saw an enormous frame church, which I concluded was Mennonite before I even saw the sign. We were approaching Goessel and the Mennonite museum.

The museum was spread out over several buildings and was actually more genealogy than history, but it was interesting and fun. An attendant tried his best to contain his curiosity. Obviously a farmer, his suit did not come from Brooks Brothers, and he seemed ill at ease in it. He wondered what we were doing in Goessel. As soon as I said we were researching the Santa Fe Trail, he questioned no more.

After dinner in McPherson I convinced Betty that a walk over the overpass toward the business district would be just the ticket for losing any weight put on by the dinner. As we walked, the roadway climbed higher and higher over the railroad tracks and the walkway grew narrower and narrower. At the top Betty developed a case of acrophobia. I told her she could get over it by walking on the guardrail over the chasm forty feet below, but she remained unconvinced and tiptoed the remaining distance with her eyes closed.

Monday, April 4, 1988

The plans were to meet Jere, Leo, and Bonita at the Red Coach Inn restaurant at 7:30 this morning. There we outlined the plan for the day and were joined by Bob Gray, our guide for this stretch of the trail.

We had heard that Donald Cress might join us this morning as he was eager to learn a little more about the trail. Sure enough, when we arrived at Meier's Food and Fuel in Durham, the assembly point, there was his brown pickup. Good thing, too, as we would need those four claws before sundown. Donald was with his wife, Doris, a delightful woman.

A young couple, Ken and Iralee Barnard, also came along. He is in charge of the flight department at a local college and has a Cessna 150. She is a botanist and photographer, who has shot many trail ruts from their plane. Also in the party was Dennis Youk, who lives nearby.

We divided into groups. I left the Chrysler at the cafe and rode in the back of Donald's pickup. And as I did, I wondered about whatever possessed me, so long ago, to so dedicate myself to the geography of the western historic trails. Had I not done so I would be back in St. Louis today, jockeying a desk, trying to make a public relations client happy by grinding out insipid press releases.

Instead, here I was with the wind in my face, bouncing through the fields in the bed of a pickup truck under an opalescent Kansas sky laced with slender contrails, surrounded by the sights and smells of a century ago. Good friends were around me and I had attained some measure of respect as a trail geographer and historian. Could a life be more satisfying?

At the Cottonwood Crossing we found another set of ruts. Bob Gray said this is where Susan Magoffin stopped to pick plums with her maid during her historic sojourn in 1846. Well, almost. It is where she looked at the plums, bemoaned the fact that they were unripe, and picked gooseberries instead.

We took off to find the "blowout." This was new to me. It's a place where wagon wheels destroyed the turf and the Kansas wind took over to blow out the trail, eroding it with air instead of water. The cut was astounding! Perhaps a dozen feet deep in places. Leo, Bonita, and Jere decided to hoof it to the next section. We walked back to the trucks and drove north, west, and then south to the point where the road meets the trail.

We went back to Meier's Cafe for lunch. I had been thinking about their bierocks all morning—delicious pastries filled with meat and sauerkraut. But they were served only on Thursdays, so we were out of luck.

Afterwards we headed toward McPherson county in search of the grave of young Ed Miller. The eighteen-year-old boy was riding to a ranch near here to bring news of a relative's illness and rode into an ambush. Those at the ranch knew the Indians were rampaging and were holed up there. Through a telescope they watched the Indians circling a single rider. He disappeared.

A few days later soldiers rescued the ranch family and

The grave of Ed Miller

they all went in search of Miller. About fifty yards from the trail they found his body in the weeds, scalped, shot with arrows, and speared. They wrapped him in a blanket, carried him to the nearby knoll, and buried him.

Early in the day we learned that Bob Gray has a cause. A granite marker at the spot where the Sibley party treated with the Kansa Indians in August 1825 was moved to Highway 153, just southeast of Elyria where there is also a turnout and a KSHS marker. Bob is right; moving it was a dopey thing to do.

We went west of town, to the point where the treaty was actually made. Bob has placed a small granite marker there, along the north side of the road. The trouble is, his inscription is off by two months and forty years. (It reads "June 1865.") We all agreed that the original marker, moved by well-meaning but ill-advised people, should be returned to the correct site.

Near the Rice County line we came to the farm of Jim and Mim Nelson. Mim took us into the pasture behind her barn where we mudded out to four nice swales. Some prize pigs, a cow or two, and a few horses watched us with little enthusiasm.

After getting permission from the Kansas Horizon Oil Company we explored the ruts on their land that led to the Little Arkansas. A dirt road took us into a field alongside an irrigation reservoir. In front of us were four swales leading down toward the river. We followed them on foot a short distance until they petered out. Then it was back to the highway.

We took another foray into military history. Arriving at the well-marked site of Camp Grierson, we followed a dirt road into a picnic area. There a number of soldiers had been garrisoned. The sign says that George Custer was here; Leo says no way. We believe Leo. Custer, like Jesse James, has the reputation for being many places where he couldn't or wouldn't have gone.

The sign also explains that the depressions in the turf were left when the graves of some fifteen soldiers were disinterred and the bodies moved to Fort Leavenworth. The graves evidently were left open and gradually the grass has covered the area. Now people eat potato salad and watermelon in those gravesites. Gave me a chill to think about it.

At the crossing of the Little Arkansas, we took a probe in Donald's pickup. There were seven people in the bed of the truck now. We would need that weight.

We crossed the Little Ark on the main road and headed down the bank on a dirt lane for perhaps a half mile. The pickup nosed down toward a swale—the trail! Heading right for the river. On foot we slithered along the bank of the swale. Before us stood the most enormous cottonwood I had ever seen. It was aligned with the rut swale, which turned to the left to go around it, so it had to have been there in trail days. We saw a DAR marker on the opposite bank, but no evidence of a crossing. In times of low water, we were told, the stones thrown in the bed by the soldiers can be seen, but this was not low water.

Instead of backing out, Donald decided to go out in the stubble to loop around toward the road, a nearly fatal error. All four tires spun rapidly, sending showers of mud skyward. But somehow we kept moving. And gradually we regained the old roadway. It was well past dinner time when we headed back to McPherson.

We were in a hurry to get back. It was the night of the NCA basketball championship, underdog Kansas U. vs. Oklahoma. The Jayhawks came out on the court in a dead run and never let up. The Sooners gave them a good game and there were more than a few breath-holding moments. When Kansas won, we expected the town to erupt into a celebration. It didn't. There was nothing but silence— except for one lone car that circled the motel, with the driver honking in jubilation.

On the second go-around, a Kansas highway patrolman cut off the driver. He tried to back up. Another patrol car neatly pulled in behind him. An officer asked to see his drivers' license. Printed clearly on the license was the name: Jere Krakow. No, he was not an alum. Lengthy explanations followed, but it was obvious that Jere wasn't tanked— despite that six-pack he'd had with his pizza. He went back to his room with a warning (and a little-boy grin).

Tuesday, April 5, 1988

The weather turned cold and the wind revved up several knots. We drove directly to Ralph's Ruts after breakfast. Ralph is Ralph Hathaway, who lives four miles west and a mile north of Chase. I had been to his place in September, when a busload of conferees visited from Hutchinson. Quiet, soft-spoken, and very cognizant of history, Ralph gave us a quick background of his place. He is the third generation to farm the 420-acre spread.

We got in his van to tour his ruts. Beautiful swales! Last year, with the help of Marc Simmons, Ralph learned that

Ralph's Ruts

the three people killed on the property in 1867 were the mother-in-law of Franz Huning, her son, and their driver—ambushed by Charlie Bent's renegade Cheyennes and Arapahos. Ralph deduced where their wagon would have been mired in sand, following the memoirs of Franz Huning. It was exactly where he had found many pieces of broken crockery years earlier.

We went west to the site of the Plum Buttes, which were three enormous mountains of sand blown out from the riverbed that served as sentinels during trail days. Over the years (perhaps only twenty) the wind destroyed its own creation. Ralph's father told Ralph that as a boy he could see the remaining butte from the ranch house. It was only about thirty feet high when Ralph was growing up. Now there is nothing in that section but broken land.

We decided to return to the Little Arkansas for more exploration. The wind was a killer. It was cold and damp. The steering wheel of the Chrysler was crabbed fifteen degrees to keep the car on the pavement.

By the time we arrived at the county line it was spitting rain. Leo, Bonita, and Jere hiked through the wheat—some six inches high—to the riverbank. Betty and I, being much more sensible, stayed in the car. They searched for more than an hour, finding some evidence of a crossing, but not the stone from the old bridge abutments which they had sought.

Looking to the southeast from the car, I could see in my mind's eye the great stone corral that once stood there. It must have been an amazing structure. Two hundred feet by four hundred feet, several feet high, fifteen inches thick. And not a pebble left today. The rancher who owned it sold off all the rock in the latter part of the nineteenth century. A stone school a mile south and a half mile west is all that remains. Our later examination revealed that it is stuccoed over.

When the three explorers returned to the Chrysler, we headed west to Great Bend. After a quick look at Fort Zarah State Park, we picked up Bob Button. Button is quiet but very sharp and very careful. An amateur archaeologist, he had helped excavate the two sites of Fort Zarah. One is east of the park a half mile; the other a half mile south of there, on the bank of Walnut Creek.

The bank of Walnut Creek is the site of another major archaeological dig, the Allison-Peacock trading post. Fighting the howling wind, we discovered that the stone foundations are still there. Across the creek is the site of the postal station. We found the swale leading down to the river from the high ground, but it is strewn with gigantic logs. We skirted it, looking for evidence of the log pilings in the riverbed which supported the toll bridge from trail days. Either the water is too high or the piles are completely gone.

Wednesday, April 6, 1988

The wind seemed to have had its fun yesterday and was somewhat quieter. But it was cold. I put on a heavy plaid shirt, a battle jacket, and my heavy winter coat. By the end of the day we had the air conditioner on and I wished I had worn a short-sleeved shirt.

We were heading into the Kansas sun by 8:40 A.M. U.S. 56 looks more like a highway of the 1940s than the 1980s. The pavement is quite narrow, it has virtually no shoulder, and there's lots of grass on either side. So much less monotonous, I think, than the interstates. The road ran northeast at this point and I could see the electric poles along the section lines transform themselves with each mile. As my line of sight aligned with them, the wires turned to gleaming silver strands and the sun passed through the insulators with a special luminosity. Kansas is a good place to be in the morning.

Beside us was the railroad which had killed the Santa Fe Trail—the Atchison, Topeka & Santa Fe.

Yesterday the windmills were all canted with the wind, their tail vanes parallel with the plane of the fans. The wind was blowing so hard that the vanes were turning anyway.

Pawnee Rock

This day was calm, resting before another onslaught. Leo told us that he is so used to being buffeted by the wind that one day when it didn't blow, he walked out of his house and fell down.

With us was George Elmore, a Fort Larned ranger and former student of Leo's. Our first point of call was Pawnee Rock. I first saw it in 1958, when Don Marshall and I stopped there on the way back from a quick tour of the West. It was a romantic spot then for me. I imagined what had happened there in the age of the Pawnee, before the rock was truncated by stonecutters. (The antique shop on the corner of Centre Street and U.S. 56 has some walls made of stone quarried from Pawnee Rock.)

I came by it a second time last September, when a bus full of conferees from the Hutchinson symposium of the SFTA managed to squeeze through the entry and drive to the top. That time I thought the place was corny.

This time was like the first. The sun was hitting it full

in the face. There is a concrete pavilion on top. George thinks the rock once was as high as the roof of that pavilion, maybe higher. I think it was a whole lot higher myself, but someone certainly should triangulate the old pictures so we'd know for certain. I used the iron circular stair to get to the top and looked to the northeast to see the faint trace of the trail alongside. Then I looked back and could see the trail moving over Ash Creek and toward Fort Larned. It's been said that the garrison flag there could be seen from the top of the rock.

A woman in her sixties drove up in an old Plymouth. Overcome with curiosity, she asked what we were doing there. I told her. Uninvited, she proceeded to give us the history of the rock and of the trail, in very sketchy terms. Then she said, "But you folks probably know as much about it as I do." Let us hope so; let us hope so.

She was waiting for the sun to hit a small wildflower. She told us that there are more than forty different kinds of wildflowers on Pawnee Rock and she had pictures of all of them.

We headed back to the southwest. George was a little confused by some detours, but after zigging and zagging over county roads, we reached the site of the Ash Creek Crossing. This is the point where Susan Magoffin's carriage overturned, crashing on top of her. In order to free another acre of ground for cultivation, the rancher diked up both banks of the creek, thus obliterating forever the swales that led down to and out of the crossing.

Just as we were about to leave the site, a fellow named Ed Boyd drove by in a pickup, waved to George, and braked to a halt. He wanted to know what was going on

Clay Ward

The Ash Creek Crossing in 1947

and got the standard answer. He told us he had some pretty good pictures of the crossing taken in 1947 before it was bladed out. Newspaper photographer Clay Ward had given them to him. When we said we'd like to see them, he offered to go home and get them.

A few minutes later he returned with two sharp, mounted prints. There was a beautiful swale going in and another coming out, photographed from both sides of the creek. We were delighted with the find and copied them.

At Larned we drove through the city streets to see the sights, including a limestone bluff overlooking the river. It is now topped with an elegant house. In trail days it was

The Pawnee Fork was negotiated where the small bridge at left crosses today.

topped with Indians.

Next was the Larned Cemetery. The connection between cemeteries and the SFT is interesting. Once a site is filled with bodies, it is unlikely that it will be cultivated. Hence, the land contours remain as they were. Ruts once on that ground stay visible. So it is with the Larned Cemetery. Along the east edge, looking north, we could see a number of slight depressions indicating the presence of the trail.

The water tower at the state hospital was our next landmark. We saw its silver bulb from atop Pawnee Rock. Mounting the eminence we were taken with a sweeping view. This is the kind of vista Fremont must have been given when he climbed the Blue Mound on the Oregon

Trail. Now I could see the flag at Fort Larned, more than five miles west. Below us twisted the Pawnee Fork, and just west of its first bend was the site of the Boyd Ranch, which had been a place of prostitution. Four women were counted there in the 1872 census, one of whom was black. A small building housed a barroom; behind it small cribs lined the hall.

About a mile away we passed a series of dugouts. Some historians believe this spot to be the location of the first military post, which lasted only a few months toward the end of 1859. It was called Camp on Pawnee Fork and was also known as Camp Alert. Right next to the quarry which supplied the sandstone to build Fort Larned is a contemporary quarry, where the stone was obtained for the newly reconstructed blockhouse.

That's where we went next—to wonderful old Fort Larned, where the National Park Service has done such a magnificent job of reconstruction. The fort was of commanding importance to the Santa Fe trade beginning in 1860 and was abandoned in 1878, a few years after the subjugation of the Indians. Soon afterward it was sold and converted into a ranching operation. It served in that capacity until the 1960s, when it was acquired by the NPS, and the long, meticulous job of restoration began.

When I visited in September it was virtually complete, with nothing remaining to be done but the reconstruction of the blockhouse. When we passed by it in March, I noticed that even that had been completed. This was my first closeup view.

George marched the rest of our troops right to it, but I circled it with my cameras. I have never seen a better

Fort Larned

job of reconstruction. Inside the building I noticed the loopholes which perforated the walls were tapered in a wedge-shaped profile toward the interior, allowing the riflemen to swing their guns to the left or right. There was a platform halfway up, from which a second group of men could fire.

As it turned out, the building was not needed for the defense of the fort, for it was never attacked. So it was used as a jail. A trapdoor led to an excavated area below, little bigger than a crawl space. That was the solitary confinement area. A passageway leads to a well, which is accessible only from the blockhouse. On the main floor is a wood structure shaped a little like an upright coffin—a sweatbox. There is evidence, said George, that men were also hanged by their thumbs.

George led the group up a slender ladder some twenty feet near the peak of the hexagonal roof. The roof was crowned with a tall cupola, the sentry box.

George led us down a mowed swath in the prairie, the "history trail." Is it ever! We passed the prairie laden with native grasses, now awaiting the warm sun of spring. We saw the site of the mail station, which predated construction of the fort, being active in 1858.

It didn't take much imagination to fancy myself a trader approaching the fort from the southwest. I could hear the distant sound of a bugle, and could see the men near the parade. They lived by the hour, these soldiers did, never knowing when they would be called out to escort a caravan through a land populated by hostiles. The white man was killing off a lot of game as he passed through, and the Indians were in mortal danger. Starvation awaited them if they couldn't stop the advance. Worse was the threat of life on a reservation. The Indians retaliated, and the government responded with force.

Sympathy toward the plight of the Indian was hard to come by in the 1860s, as they resorted to atrocities in an attempt to frighten the whites from ancestral lands. The Indian was referred to derisively as "Lo," as in "Lo, the noble savage," a phrase often used by white sympathizers of the Indian predicament. The Indians were in the right place in the wrong century. Had they been contemporaneous with today's society, their rights would have been protected by the courts and the rest of us would be in a hell of a mess.

At the Santa Fe Trail Center, we delivered our greetings to Ruth Olson, the young, pretty executive director of the center. Historians here were in a quandary in the 1960s. The Pawnee County Historical Society had taken over the Fort Larned buildings and used many to house their extensive collection of contributed artifacts. Restoration of the fort clearly would cost far more than the county could afford. It was a job for the feds. And when the feds indeed took over the place, they insisted that the society take its stuff elsewhere. Evidently not too tactfully.

So some rather substantial amounts of money were contributed toward the construction of the Santa Fe Trail Center to house the exhibits which had been at Fort Larned. There probably is still too much here, but the exhibits please the visitors.

At the "detached site" of Fort Larned, a branch of the trail swung to the south to connect with the wet route on the Arkansas. Seven rut swales are all that remain of this road.

Following close by that road we reached Highway 56 at Garfield and turned right, continuing on for a couple of miles to the site of Coon Creek. There was what we had hoped to see at Ash Creek earlier in the day—a series of swales leading down into and out of the creek.

George is a military historian—that figures, since he was Leo's student and Leo is the outstanding military historian in the state. So he took us to a site which he feels had great importance in the Indian wars.

We turned down a two-track and lurched beneath a high tension line, passing over broken ground to a mesa which was the location of a onetime Sioux-Cheyenne village. In 1867 there were 300 lodges, perhaps 1,500 men, women, and children.

Gen. Winfield S. Hancock, George Custer, and 1,400 men with artillery were also here, stalking them. From the ridge which we had observed a few miles back to the east, they saw the Sioux and Cheyenne in full battle regalia, ready to fight. Indian agents stepped in and calmed things down for a while.

Then Hancock, itching for a fight, encircled the place. The Indians pulled out hurriedly and stealthily, leaving some horses and an old man to tend the fires, making it appear as if the village were still occupied. That night Custer crawled into the village on his hands and knees and found it deserted. The next day troops moved in. An inventory was taken and the list still survives. When they fled, the Indians left virtually everything. The whites also found a young white girl whom they claimed had been repeatedly raped.

Hancock and the infantry camped here for several days while Custer went out in pursuit of the Indians. Custer reported back that the mail station on the Smoky Hill River had been burned. In retaliation Hancock ordered everything in the village burned. (This story is covered in Custer's *My Life on the Plains*. It also appeared in *Harper's Illustrated Weekly* in 1867.)

Our research day over, we headed back over dirt and gravel roads some thirty miles to Larned. We passed rows of abandoned stone fenceposts, so typical of western Kansas—still standing but now backed by modern fences with steel posts. Frequently there are no fences at all; just stands of wheat, now turning from lime green to emerald. That soaker which blessed the fields a few days ago was beneficent to the ranchers as well. I imagine the wheat will be sixteen inches high before this job is finished, and it will have been turned into bread before the map book leaves the presses this fall.

Thursday, April 7, 1988

Today didn't start out very well. I misplaced my map of Edwards County. I was sure it had blown away—the wind gusts are strong enough to blow half of Kansas away. Fortunately, Lisa had copies in St. Louis, but I would have felt a lot more comfortable if some Little Person snuck up behind me and tucked it in my shorts. (After an hour of grousing about the loss, it turned up in plain sight on the bed.)

After breakfast we took off toward the site of the Battle of Coon Creek. When we arrived at the historical marker, Leo told us it was on the wrong side of the river. The sign had some interesting material—the first reference I had seen to homosexuality in an Indian nation. It describes the amazement of the soldiers who witnessed a tall Indian woman, called the "queen" of the tribe, who passed among the ranks of the defeated Indian braves issuing orders for the disposition of the wounded. She was dressed in ornate tribal regalia.

Leo said this was actually a homosexual in drag, that homosexuals were rather highly regarded in the Comanche nation. Betty challenged this, saying that feminine men, especially transvestites, would indeed have been highly regarded, but that a masculine-appearing gay brave would not have been. Feminine men were thought to have stronger ties to the spirit world.

We drove to the Boot Hill Museum in Dodge City. This is a beautiful presentation, I think, although I have heard nothing but unfortunate remarks about the hokiness of Dodge City. It appears to be an old hotel, and a visitor must enter and pay admission to get to "Front Street," a row of false-front buildings depicting Dodge in the cowtown days.

Next we drove to the Kansas Heritage Center. This is sort of a city-county historical society focused upon the schools. Here we were joined by Betty Braddock, the director, and Noel Ary, assistant director of the center. Noel had pulled out all the USDA aerial photographs of the county for us. We scrambled over each other trying to read them spread out on the floor. This is how the ruts had looked in 1938! We spotted ruts near the town of Ford and also those west of Dodge. Then we took off in search of them.

We could find the ruts at Ford easily, for there is a fine little map in Marc Simmons's book, and the landmarks he uses brought us precisely to the right location. Across the road is a line of wooden fenceposts, each of them topped with a worn-out cowboy boot.

On the way back to Dodge, Betty Braddock conducted our two-car caravan on a guided tour of old Fort Dodge, just east of town. For a change, the radios connecting our cars worked well.

We reentered Dodge City on "P" Street, off Wyatt Earp Boulevard, the main drag. Betty Braddock told the story of a saloon owner who appeared before the city council to petition for the renaming of P Street. When asked why, he said, "How would you like to be selling beer on the corner of P and Earp?"

She directed us to some ruts east of town. Leo doubted their authenticity. They aligned with nothing on my maps, so we dismissed them and went to lunch at El Charro.

Betty Burnett and I had visited the fabled ruts west of Dodge a couple of months ago, and were puzzled that we could find no trace. That was near the start of our Santa Fe Trail adventures, when I was really looking for Oregon Trail-type ruts—sharp two-tracks. To date I have found no such thing on the SFT, just grassy, linear depressions. Those west of Dodge are quite faint, but this time, with the help of our guides, I saw them. And again I photographed them, knowing all the while that the pictures will be utterly useless, because ruts like this do not show up well in color and never in black-and-white. Perhaps in another month, after the buffalo grass has greened up a little, we can try again. Then maybe something will show, on the color film at least.

A newspaper reporter and a photographer from the Dodge City paper joined us there and wanted an interview and some pictures. (A week or so later we saw the result. Betty was described as the publisher of Patrice Press and I, the editor! Also she was the only one of the three Ph.D.'s who got a "Dr." in front of her name. Don't know who she knows, but I wish she'd introduce me.)

We passed the site of another "point of rocks" referred to by the traders. That makes three of them in the state of Kansas. Well, two now, for this one was blasted away by the local highway department in 1981 for the widening of U.S. 50. How could they escape the lash of public opinion over that? Gone forever, because of the edict of some insensitive jerk!

The SFTA—and all historic preservation organizations —needs a committee charged with assembling dishonor rolls, listing the names of the klutzes who destroy famous places for dumb reasons. Those names should be included right on the historical markers.

Nearby, according to the marker beside the road, were ''The Caches,'' where an early trader buried his goods after his mules perished during a severe blizzard. The Caches evidently were large excavations in the earth beneath a relatively small opening. And they have simply disappeared. How could that be? Surely there must be some evidence somewhere. I wonder if the SFTA could appoint an investigative committee to try to determine the precise location. Can we be content without knowing this?

We returned Betty Braddock and Noel to Dodge City and then headed west toward the town of Cimarron. Just before reaching the Arkansas River is the Cimarron Crossing Park. Leo told us there that more traders turned southwest in this vicinity—the ''Middle Crossings''—than all the other alternates combined, including the Mountain Branch. The crossing marked on the 1850s maps is about a mile and a half upstream. We were told that there is nothing to see there.

We had trouble as soon as we tried to leave the park. Leo and Bonita had been towing their Nissan pickup behind their motor home. Now the starter of the motor home wouldn't engage. Leo crawled underneath the engine and worked for perhaps a half hour, trying to jar the solenoid loose, while Bonita worked the switch in the cab. No luck. We decided to disengage the pickup and chain it to the front of the motor home so David could pull Goliath. An hour or so later Bonita returned to the campground in the pickup. The ignition switch finally worked. Leo was right behind her in the motor home. He vowed that the engine would not be turned off until we were through for the night.

At last we headed west out of Cimarron, the motor home in front, Bonita second, then Jere, then Betty and me. Suddenly Jere braked and pulled over to the side. "Gregory, I missed my corner," he told us over the radio. "You go on ahead."

What corner? We drove ahead, expecting that Leo and Bonita had already done so, but there was no sign of them. As we passed the mile-long Ingalls feed lot, the stench made our eyes water. "Jere, where are you? What's going on?" I radioed every few minutes. No response. I figured there was no way those radio waves could get through that aroma.

After waiting at a rest area for a long while, I turned into town, calling Jere almost nonstop. Suddenly Bonita came on the air. "Jere's making a phone call," she said. "We're at the bank in Ingalls. I just walked past the car, heard the radio popping, and decided to answer it." We topped a rise in Ingalls and there they were—the motor home, the Nissan, and the Taurus. Somehow we had missed learning that Jere needed to contact some folks here.

In his conversation with town residents, Jere learned that the DAR marker across the road from the Ingalls Museum (an old depot) had once been up on the highway, but had been moved to town because of vandalism. Folks thought it would be safer in town. That's a shame. It's hard to do much damage to a great granite boulder. They should have left it alone.

One of Jere's calls was to Dale Eichenauer, who ranches

seven miles south and seven miles west of Ingalls. He had some ruts on his place and was very willing to show us around.

Dale met us with a warm welcome. He is about six feet two, skinny, and as typical a rancher as any I have ever seen—independent as hell and used to hard work. He's also deeply interested in the history of the area. He said his interest came on fairly recently and he wished he'd paid more attention to the subject in school.

Dale's father bought this ground in 1929. Dale remembers seeing the ruts along the east side of section 34, where the wagon wheels had so compacted the soil that the ruts are actually reversed. The wind blew out the sand everywhere else, so the wagon tracks stood up higher than the surrounding prairie.

Hobart Stocking evidently had been here, because Dale remembered ''some fellow from Oklahoma'' coming to the farm to examine the trail.

Dale took us into a pasture behind an old schoolhouse. It was the very building where he'd learned the Three R's. He had such good memories of those days, he bought the place and moved it to his land as a souvenir.

We could see an enormous bull in the next pasture. ''If you can cross that pasture in 2.9 seconds, go ahead and do it,'' Dale said. ''But the bull can do it in 2.10.''

Dale had dug out a trench silo in the dirt in that pasture. This is a cut perhaps twenty feet across, six feet deep, and fifty yards long. About three feet down a line is visible which is darker than the surrounding soil. It contrasts with the color of the excavated soil, which has been piled on top of the bank. The black line of the former surfaces dips right

Dale Eichenauer's trench silo

in the middle of the cut and is aligned with the gentle swales on either side of the uncut ground. The compaction caused by the trail couldn't be more perfectly shown.

We got into Dale's pickup and rode a mile east, then turned up a roadless section line, lurched another mile north and parked. After walking for a half mile over the rolling prairie, we found eight or nine fine rut swales through that pasture, right on the Stocking route. This route crossed the Arkansas at the smelly Ingalls feedlot and aligned perfectly with what we had just seen.

Dale had told us that he used bronze divining rods to locate metal. In fact, he had turned up two old ox chains in his fields, buried five feet down with other artifacts and

Dale Eichenauer and his ox chains

lots of char. One chain is eight feet long and the other is ten. He showed us these and other wagon parts he had dug up. I wanted to see the rods, which were actually welding rods. I had one question, "Do they work?"

"Try them," he said, handing them to me. They are about four feet long and a quarter-inch in diameter. The ends had been bent to ninety-degree angles for grips. Dale rolled a steel pipe on the ground and asked me to walk slowly toward it. I held the rods straight out in front of me about four inches apart. As I passed over the pipe, the rods came together and crossed in the shape of an X. I could feel the pull—it was truly magnetic—despite my trying to keep the rods apart. My skepticism evaporated, but I still couldn't explain what was going on. The others tried it and the same thing happened each time.

Friday, April 8, 1988

As soon as we finished breakfast Paul Bentrup arrived. Paul ranks right up there with Les Vilda as a Santa Fe Trail ambassador. In fact, he received the same award at Hutchinson. A wonderfully vigorous guy of seventy-one, Bentrup is old-worldly in his language and voice inflections. He reminds me of W. C. Fields, except that there is nothing fraudulent about Paul. He is a genuine philosopher, a lover of knowledge and a lover of people. We headed east toward Pierceville in search of the nun's grave.

This quest (for the Holy Grail, as Paul puts it) began for me in Hutchinson last September, after hearing a fascinating talk by Mary Jean Cook. She has been searching for the grave of Sr. Mary Alphonsa Thompson, who died in 1867 while on the trail with Bishop Jean Baptiste Lamy and two other Sisters of Loretto. The eighteen-year-old apparently succumbed to cholera or fright after a prolonged Indian battle at the Arkansas Crossing. A photograph purported to be taken after the burial shows the other two nuns kneeling at the grave, as the bishop and his entourage prepare to resume their journey to Santa Fe.

I think the photograph was staged after the event, although I don't know why anyone would do that. Many questions must be answered before I can believe it is authentic. Who was the photographer? Why is the presence of a photographer not mentioned in any accounts of the event? Glass plates were used at that time and had to be sensitized and developed immediately, before the emulsion dried. Was a dark tent set up in the middle of the battle? Or immediately after, when Lamy was in such a hurry to move on? In that desert country, where was the necessary water obtained? Why don't other photographs of this same trip survive? Why is the vegetation in the picture more like that of New Mexico than that of Kansas?

Many historians, both amateur and professional, have been trying to find the grave, based upon the photograph and the several accounts of the incident. Paul feels it is at Point of Rocks. Not the one in New Mexico or the one in southern Kansas or the one west of Dodge City, but the one west of Pierceville.

We took the road that runs next to the railroad tracks, a good bit of which covers the SFT. About 3.5 miles west is an outcropping on the north side of the tracks—another Point of Rocks. Paul has studied its characteristics thoroughly over the years and is convinced this is the site of the burial.

And that is as far as we can go with that subject, because no sign of a grave remains, although Paul Horgan, in his *Lamy of Santa Fe,* implies that the grave location was known in recent years. We concluded that we had better importune Dale Eichenauer to get up here with his witching rods. Maybe a search party could take about three lineal feet apiece and walk over a stretch of a couple of miles, each with two bronze rods.

Will the Sister's grave ever be found? Perhaps not in Paul's lifetime; perhaps not in mine. But so long as there are people around who have the same enthusiasm as Paul Bentrup has, there is a strong chance that someday the grave will be found. His zeal inspires others to keep searching. I just hope we both will be there when it happens.

We walked down the railroad tracks for perhaps a hundred yards enveloped in silence. There was a stillness about the land which was broken only by the sighing of the wind. It wasn't a howl or a whine or a moan—it had a friendlier sound.

Is this the place called Pawnee Fort? We came across a ramshackle log structure out in the flat by the river. I don't know what it is. No one with us knows either.

We went next to the ranch of Harley M. Foulks, who is the manager of the Garden City co-op. As we walked out in the pasture, Paul told me about a friend of his, Ramona Webster Kessler, who grew up in the area. She said that when she was a youngster, there was a certain place in her pasture where the milk cows would not go. It was close to the line fence in section 31. Could that have been the location of the nun's grave? Paul can't get it off his mind. We stopped in front of the site where there is a tall mound of earth, perhaps fifteen feet high, some thirty yards out into the field. Paul has searched the area and found nothing.

I wished we could have met Harley M. Foulks. For our benefit he mowed a swath through his pasture, where the weeds from last fall were still two to three feet tall, to the point where half a dozen ruts are. Then he crossed back and forth over the ruts with the mower so we could see them and walk over them easily. Obviously, Harley isn't going to mow for everyone who wants to see his ruts, so I took a bearing from the oil well in the field—120 degrees, and about 300 yards away.

After lunch we headed west to Deerfield and Paul's ruts. He has some good swales on his ranch, about two and one-half miles west of Deerfield and has deeded the ten-acre plot where they're located to the Kearny County Museum. The Kansas State Historical Society is ready to mount a sign there explaining their significance. Good for Paul. That's what I call sharing.

While we were at the site we were joined by Linda Peters, a schoolteacher who had gone on one of Leo's guided tours. Her principal was happy to give her the time off. Obviously this is a worthy cause.

We headed south in search of the Wagon Bed Spring. While Betty and I were in Santa Fe last fall, we had had breakfast with Marc Simmons, who told us exactly how to get to the spring and even sketched a map explaining it. Following his directions, I walked the Cimarron for more than a mile and failed to find it. I concluded that someone had stolen the marker.

Leo hadn't seen the site recently and thought I could be right. Before approaching the spring we stopped in the Kearny County Museum at Ulysses, another remarkable local museum, to meet Fern Basire, who grew up just a mile or two from the spring. She said that we couldn't drive anywhere near it; we would have to walk in.

We were joined then by Ron and Karla French. Ron said we certainly could drive to the spring and led the way south over gravel and dirt roads. We drove within a few feet of the DAR marker. Had there not been a heavy rain the night before we could have gone even those last few yards. So it did exist; it hadn't been stolen. But I had completely misunderstood Marc's directions. I don't think we could have been talking about the same place.

As it was, we walked the short distance to the marker, then walked on another quarter of a mile to what had been a spring, but now was only an ugly hole in the ground.

Many trail historians are convinced that this is the real location of Wagon Bed Spring, so the DAR rock is slated to be moved to that site soon.

We returned to the highway, went across the bridge over the Cimarron and up to the high ground. At a pullout near a series of markers, with the help of Ron's directions and binoculars, we were able to establish a bearing of 246 degrees from the marker at Wagon Bed Spring, a good two miles to the southwest.

Back at Lakin we stopped to pick up Pat Heath, Linda Peters' mother. Linda, her husband, Bruce, and their two sons also joined our caravan in a new Suburban. We took a rugged gravel road north of the railroad tracks which eventually brought us to Indian Mound, a tall earthen struc-

Jere Krakow, left, and Pat Heath atop Indian Mound, overlooking Chouteau's Island.

ture overlooking Chouteau's Island. There, while dark clouds gathered and lightning punctuated her words, Pat gave us a history of the place. It was probably made as a lookout by early traders. From there Indians could be spotted, as well as caravans taking the Cimarron Cutoff and crossing the Arkansas River at the east end of the island. A biting wind chased us back into the cars and a few raindrops gave us a hint of a big storm to come.

At a particularly rough stretch we decided to leave the Chrysler and head across country in the Peters' Suburban. After rigorous jouncing, we found some wonderful continuous rut swales. This was another "segment" that we could record.

Then, as the light was leaving us, we quit for the day. Driving east, back to Lakin, we watched the show up ahead. The front had passed through rapidly, giving us only scattered rain. Although the western sky was beginning to clear, a powerful storm was building in the east. Lightning raced from cloud to cloud, crackling every few seconds. Thunder boomed in the distance. Probably by now the storm was listing hail on its manifest.

Darkness had nearly enveloped us when three mule deer bounded across our path, heading north. They gained the top of the hill and stopped, looking down at us. They made a dramatic silhouette against the northwestern sky.

"What a shot!" exclaimed Bruce.

Betty rolled her eyes. He wasn't talking about a camera.

Saturday, April 9, 1988

Paul Bentup joined us again as we headed west on Highway 50. It was cold, but I didn't expect to see snow still lingering in the ditches after the warm spell earlier in the week. On Palm Sunday this area had a record blizzard—two feet of snow was dumped on some places.

The Santa Fe Railroad paralleled our highway on the left. We turned off the pavement and vaulted over the tracks on such a steep incline that the road ahead was obscured by the hood of the car. The Arkansas River was less than a mile ahead of us. We followed the twisting road to an old farm. A DAR marker was in the yard; the house was abandoned. We were at the site of old Fort Aubry, in use less than a year and named for (not founded by) Francis

X. Aubry, after his death.

We walked around the barn and along the bank of a healthy-looking creek to some depressions in the earth, perhaps eight feet in diameter and maybe six inches deep. Paul told us these were rifle pits. There were several on this side of the creek; more on the other side. What happened to the buildings nobody knows, but at one time there were some here.

We drove through Syracuse, then a dozen miles farther west to the alleged (by Paul) site of Pretty Encampment. What a wimpy name for a military post! Lewis Garrard was there in 1846 when it was a campground. He stopped there again on his return the following year. The area is pretty, no doubt about that. We were overlooking a broad plain. A rushing creek was in the foreground and across the Arkansas River to the south were sand hills.

Paul said the stage station had been abandoned in 1871, after which the Indians burned it. But there is serious dispute about where it was.

We continued west along the Mountain Branch into Colorado. Some of our sources say that the trail jogged a mile to the north as it enters what is now Colorado, but we couldn't understand why. Terrain, probably. Certainly the teamsters had a better perception of things from the side of an ox than we do from the seat of a Chrysler.

We drove northeast of Holly to the cemetery where there are some good swales. Paul slipped through the fence to point them out to us. What energy he has!

We passed through Lamar and headed toward a large sand and gravel operation—which is what brought us to Colorado today. Paul is concerned that the Carter Sand and

Gravel Company might be destroying the trail. Heavy machinery loomed on a knob to the right; a DAR marker was on the left. The land in the section back to the east had been torn up. Paul thought that they had taken some trail ruts but I couldn't see that they had. The ruts aren't very strong here anyway, but certainly we don't want to lose any more than we already have. I photographed the destruction even though we couldn't find evidence of the trail coming into or leaving the mining site. About all we can do is advise company officials where the trail is and ask them to be careful. They surely are sufficiently astute to avoid the deliberate destruction of the trail.

Jere left us at this point to drive back to Denver. The rest of us continued back to the Big Timbers Museum in Lamar, where there was a map from the 1880s showing the trail along the river through Bent County. I copied it onto my Colorado base maps. Leo found the Aubry Road leading south from the river, so I copied that too.

I wasn't crazy about tracing the Aubry route because I thought it was too specialized and not part of the "real" Santa Fe Trail. But Leo wanted to pursue it. He has made a fine study of Aubry and his record-making rides from Santa Fe to Missouri. He reminded us that Aubry's trip of five days and sixteen hours on horseback has never been duplicated.

We went back to Kansas. Earlier Paul had called David Brownlee of Syracuse, who said he would be glad to tell us about the ruts on his place some three miles east of town. We drove out there to meet a tall, smiling man with a full, untrimmed beard. He invited us into the house where we met his wife, Carol, and their two boys. As we sat around their dining room table, he drew a faint pencil line on my map of Hamilton County, showing where he thinks there are ruts of the Aubry Road.

It wasn't long before he offered to show us where they were, got in his pickup, and led the way. We found them along a fence out in a pasture. Bonita immediately started walking northeast. Leo went the other way.

When there was a break in the serious business of trail hunting, Paul entertained the two Brownlee boys (and Betty and me) with stories of his youth. When he was a young man, so he said, he was dispatched on a secret mission to the East, which took him through the dreaded Kickapoo territory. There he was captured, unfortunately with a sacred eelstone on his person. While the chiefs were debating about how to dispatch him, he was saved by a beautiful Kickapoo princess. This was fortunate, for what would we do if there were no Paul Bentrup in our midst?

Sunday, April 10, 1988

Leo took over the reins as leader and again we went after the Aubry route. We had to go it alone with the sketchy information that we had. We felt seriously handicapped by the lack of good maps. It was probe time. We had the approximate route of the trail on a sequence of maps researched some years ago, so we followed the same technique I used in researching *The Oregon Trail Revisited*. We would get on a road which intercepted the trail, drive to the point of the intercept, and look around. In this case, we found nothing for most of the day. Some of the roads were terrible, but they were dry, and, except for a little mud from the irrigation and for the awful dust that engulfed us, there were no problems.

We probed south from the ruts on David's land, southwest of the crossing of the Arkansas River. Heading down highways, then gravel roads, then dirt roads, then roads that were merely tracks. We came upon one such road with high, dead grass in the crown. It made an ominous rumbling noise as the car passed over it. In this field the wheat was growing right to the edge of the tire tracks. It was only an inch or so high there; the rest was up four to five inches.

The weather was perfect. The sky was deep blue, with scarcely any clouds. The temperature was in the sixties and the wind was down. For most of this Sunday the only things moving were our vehicles—just us against the wide Kansas sky.

"A few days ago," I radioed to Leo, "I didn't care if I ever saw another rut, but now I miss them."

"Me too."

We broke for lunch. We were then in Stanton County, just north of the county seat, Johnson City. We cruised slowly through the town and found the B&B Cafe. Inside there were perhaps a half dozen tables filled with family groups all dressed for church. The special was chicken and dumplings. It was as good as it sounds.

After lunch we brought out our maps. Since we lacked county maps for this area, we tried to put something together from USGS quads, AAA road maps, and pieces of section maps. Soon the table, large enough for eight, was covered, as we pored over the papers, trying to plot the trail into the next county.

After nearly two hours we were back on the road again,

probing through the irrigated lands. The greening had started already as the Ogallala aquifer watered the land. Huge diesel engines pumped water from that magical lake hundreds of feet below, then sent it through the enormous sprinkler systems where it was distributed over the soil.

But what was once a desert will be a desert again some day, as the great aquifer, which stretches from Minnesota to Texas, is drying up rapidly. What will these farmers do then? They don't know. They don't want to think about it either. This land was once the dreaded Jornada, and one day it will be the dreaded Jornada again.

We wound around the Bear Creek, searching for trail evidence. Leo stopped at a mobile home and knocked on the door. An elderly woman answered. She had never heard of the trail, knew nothing about any ruts nearby.

We stopped at another farmstead. Nobody home. No wonder. Among all those buildings there was no farmhouse.

At the Colorado line we turned south. Still no evidence. I had a good map of the eastern third of Baca County, so Leo suggested that I lead for a while. I went into the old familiar pattern I used in the Oregon Trail studies, citing directions and odometer readings into the tape recorder at every turn. Down the highway a mile, turn toward the trail on an intersecting road, drive to the intercept, observe, return to the highway. The pattern was repeated a dozen or more times, all without any results. The land was either under cultivation or had been recently.

We went far into Baca County, close to the Oklahoma border. Leo took over the lead again. At last Bonita thought she saw something in a tract of land to the north, as we were returning east. Leo radioed that they were going up to check it out.

Their little red pickup crossed the shallow ditch and moved up to the high ground. We stopped on the right shoulder of the gravel road to await what I thought would be another disappointing report. An old blue pickup sped by us, turned right a half mile down the road and drove to a farmstead. I guessed that the rancher was about to feed his livestock.

Leo came down from the hills, his radio crackling. "We've found something up here, Gregory, and we think you ought to come up and look it over."

The heavy Chrysler lurched across the ditch and headed up the draw behind them. There wasn't much doubt about this—we had found two and possibly three good rut swales. Bonita followed one of them on foot a quarter mile back to the northeast.

We started to leave the section. "There is a guy up here on the knob," Leo radioed. "I'm going to see if he knows anything."

It was the man in the blue pickup. I didn't try to follow. Leo soon radioed back that the fellow didn't know anything about these ruts, but he wanted us to look at something over in the next section.

I had a sheepish feeling about that. Here we were, on the man's property without his knowledge or permission. How would I feel if someone were walking around in my backyard? But instead of cussing us out, he offered to show us more of his land. Only in the West, my friend. Only in the West.

We followed him down the road a short distance and into a lane to the south. He left his truck, opened the gate, waited for us to pass through, closed the gate, and returned to his truck to continue leading the quest. A half mile into the section, he angled to the left, past a small stone building without a roof, and stopped. We did too.

I jumped from my car, hand outstretched, and introduced myself. He responded bashfully, "My name's Leon Hollen- back."

We were looking down three or four fine rut swales of the Aubry Road. They had good linearity; they were right where they were supposed to be. We were so engrossed in what we were doing that we didn't notice three horses that had come up behind the Chrysler to lick the paint.

"HEY!" Leon hollered. "GIT!" The horses ran twen- ty yards away and stopped. "They'll take the paint right off," Leon said. "And they bite, too. I've seen them bend the metal around the hood of a car. Guess they like the wax."

The Chrysler's trunk had been pretty well slobbered over, but other than a slight paint blemish, no damage was done. We turned back to the ruts. While better than anything we'd seen all day, they were not photographable. The cameras remained in the trunk, where they had been all day.

Another day's search had ended. It had been a disap- pointing day, but was crowned with a significant discovery. The sun was setting and it was time to head for Elkhart.

"Look over to your right," radioed Leo as we drove toward the town. There, against the horizon, was the celebrated landmark of the traders, the big, Kansas Point of Rocks. The last red rays in the sky backlighted it and we had a view that must have fascinated the travelers of 150 years ago. What a thrill it was for me!

Monday, April 11, 1988

I had a little surprise this morning. When we walked to the restaurant for breakfast I saw that the Chrysler was listing to port. The left rear tire was nearly flat.

The mechanic at the Phillips station found a piece of straw had penetrated the sidewall. That was from that last probe of the Aubry Trail, I'll bet.

Brooks Littrell, a guy with an outrageous Tyexus accent, met us for breakfast. He has a big Suburban, a good rig for trailing. Furthermore, it seats nine, so all of us could fit in one vehicle. No temperamental radios to worry about.

We met Edgar G. White at his law office. He is a historian as well as an attorney and has a complete file of Soil Conservation Service aerial photos of Morton County taken in 1967. Some super ruts were showing twenty-one years ago.

Next we headed for the airport. Ed has been flying since the late 1940s and has a four-seater Cessna Skylane, an ideal plane for our purposes. We took off from the Elkhart airport and headed northeast. I had the 75-200 zoom lens on the Minolta for the black-and-white work, and the regular 50mm lens on the Konica. I shot the ruts near the Cimarron with the Minolta, then fired off a slide in the Konica and moved my thumb over to wind it. Whaddayaknow— no winder! It had fallen off somewhere. There was no way to get the leverage to wind it without the winder, so that was the end of the Kodachrome for the day.

The swales we saw on the 1967 aerial photos were still very plain and photographed well. I searched for evidence of the 1856 trace, barely discernable in the 1967 pictures. I could see nothing now. Perhaps it would show with the

Ruts northeast of Elkhart, Kansas

sun lower on the horizon.

Arriving over Wagon Bed Spring I searched and searched for the marker which had given me so much trouble in March. I could tell from the channels of the Cimarron where it should be; I just couldn't see it. I shot anyway. There'd be time to study the print later.

Next we flew over the Oklahoma Panhandle; first to McNees Crossing, then over the Autograph Rocks, and finally to the location I had been waiting for—the site of Camp Nichols. And there it was, on the high point of ground between the forks of the Carrizozo creeks.

Marion Russell wrote such compelling passages about Camp Nichols, I was determined to see the place. She was allowed to go there as a bride by Kit Carson, her friend and her husband's commanding officer. Late in life she returned on a sentimental journey to find the ruin much as it is today. She stood in the depression in the earth that had been her dugout home and looked over in the direction of Carson's tent, recalling the night of a violent thunderstorm when she was alarmed by loud swearing coming from there. The tent had blown in on him and he was having trouble extricating himself.

In the 1930s Russell made a drawing of the installation as she remembered it. I have a copy. I hope one day I shall be there and stand in that depression myself.

There is a sadness associated with the site today. The owner, Austin Burdick, is about to lose it. He has been uncooperative of late and has denied permission to visit. In fact, he claimed that the Camp Nichols ruins no longer exist. On April 18 the ranch is to be auctioned away from him; some feel it will bring in excess of $20 million. I must temper my irritation with him with the knowledge that he is going through painful days. We all hope the ranch will fall into the hands of a person who appreciates its history and is willing to share it with others.

Ed greased the Cessna in to a fine landing. We helped back it into the hangar, closed the doors, and piled into the Suburban for an on-the-ground look at the Santa Fe Trail through Morton County.

First we stopped at a large steel building which houses the collections of the Morton County Historical Society. Again I had to ask myself, what is it about these Kansas counties? Why do they value local history so much? Almost every county we have stopped in has some sort of museum

A loop drive leads to a splendid overlook atop Kansas's Point of Rocks.

to mirror their heritage. They can't enjoy taxes, yet they willingly tax themselves to support such institutions. This one could be the best of all, for it is huge and has been designed as a museum, instead of being a converted school, depot, or other public building. Improvements and a new additions are being made with both tax dollars and volunteer labor.

With Brooks driving, we probed the areas we had seen from the air. The ruts we found were clean and sharp, and as expected, we failed to find any trace of the 1856 paths, less than a mile from the newer ruts. The best views were in the Cimarron National Grasslands, where the Forest Service has staked out a self-guided automobile tour for visitors.

One of the points of interest is a small enclosure around

The stone corral, spotted from Ed White's Cessna.

the graves of two children, Madge Irene Brite, 11, and Perry Merle Brite, 3. On May 1, 1914, a devastating flood poured through the area. The two children jumped from the second story of their home into the raging Cimarron in an attempt to reach their father. Their bodies were found at this site, a mile from the house, several days later.

After visiting Middle Spring we drove to the top of Point of Rocks—this the most impressive one of all. Brooks then drove us down to the flat to enable me to get some shots of the Point of Rocks as the traders would have seen it.

We continued to the Colorado border. Brooks and Ed long ago had spotted a curious enclosure from the air, which turned out to be a stone corral. They had done some research on the place and found that the site was definitely used by the military and was definitely there in trail days.

Brooks Littrell, left, and Ed White at the stone corral.

The question is, why was it so far from the wagon roads? We have no answer to that yet, but Leo has microfilms running out his ears and is the preeminent military historian of Kansas and of the Santa Fe Trail. If he can't find it, it ain't.

We said good-bye to Brooks. "We have been looking forward to this day for weeks," he exclaimed, speaking for Ed too. Although they couldn't have learned much from going over old ground with us, their joy came from sharing what they knew.

Tuesday, April 12, 1988

We parted from Leo and Bonita at the restaurant this

morning and headed east. Betty had not seen the new history museum in Topeka, so she pulled off I-70 there and I visited it again. It was as fascinating to me this time as it had been several weeks ago, when I made my first visit. "This," I said to myself, "is the way history museums ought to be."

The day was the epitome of spring. When we drove into Topeka, the redbuds were blooming and the whole town emitted the cool, gentle aroma of flowering plants. I parked on the west side of the capitol and went into the highway department building. This time I needed only the maps of Stanton County. They were missing from the original order because I didn't know we would elect to include the Aubry Road in the study.

On the way to the Kansas State Historical Society way I saw Bob Richmond plugging the parking meter beside his big Lincoln. Bob was scheduled to be honored at a seminar on Kansas history Friday and Saturday. He retired some months ago after a long and distinguished career at the Society, but today he was working again. And suddenly it all came together for me. It is because of a few dedicated guys like Bob Richmond and Joe Snell (the present director, who retires next month) that we have institutions like the history museum, which in turn inspires the county leaders to tax themselves to establish their own museums. Future generations will be able to share those thrills and grow through the values of our forebears, because of guys like Richmond and Snell.

III. APRIL 16-24, 1988

Saturday, April 16, 1988

On the road again, as Willie Nelson would say, after a week in St. Louis. Interstate 35 was afflicted with its perpetual detour west of Kansas City. The people who have kept I-70 bottled up at the state line since 1955 felt they needed to grow a little, so they expanded their operations southwestward.

At Olathe the lights of the old barbecue joint which I subsidized so heavily last month were blazing as the car plunged southwest into the darkness. Then I could see the lights of Gardner, where the Oregon Trail leaves the Santa Fe Trail, and the memories of the late 1960s flooded my mind. What happy times those were, as I probed alone, weekend after weekend, in search of the route of the Oregon Trail. Wasn't this about where I was in February 1970, when snowflakes the size of doilies began to fall? I remember fighting that storm for a few miles east of Kansas City; it was a monster. I was driving much too fast, I guess, but I knew that the storm was moving east at about thirty-five miles an hour, and if I didn't go like hell I would be driving in it for five more hours. I remember breaking out in the clear a few miles east of the Jackson County line. But it is a different Gardner today—lit up like a Christmas tree, with industry all around it.

The next sign announced Edgerton. I can remember where the Oregon Trail cut through the sections of land on both sides of that wide spot in the road. On into the blackness we headed until we reached Ottawa.

Sunday, April 17, 1988

A funny thing happened on the way to the shower; I discovered an essential part of my personal inventory was still home in the underwear drawer. We will have to find a Wal-Mart, but in the meantime, it will be two days for these skivvies.

We headed west on I-35 on this crisp, cool, clear morning. We could not have picked a better time of year for this study. The sun is bright but not hot. The humidity is low. The redbuds are a riot of color, and the deciduous trees are only now putting out their lime green leaves, soon to cover the winter blackness of the branches. The thatch on the ditches is starting to give way to the newly germinated plants below; they will do some enveloping before long. We passed vast fields of black, where the ranchers had burned off the prairie grass only weeks ago. But something is happening there too, as the color is gradually changing to green.

While I was driving, Betty was reading Adm. Richard E. Byrd's *Alone,* the story of his sojourn in Antarctica. I wish I could read while she drives, but the Kansas countryside won't let me. Nor will its history. I can see the herds of buffalo, the Pawnee and the Kansa, and the wagon trains—they are all six feet off the ground but they are there. These Great Plains are fascinating. The pioneers here experienced hardships intolerable to today's people, but they also experienced great joys, too.

East of Ottawa are rounded hills—gentle undulations that do not defy cultivation. To the west, the land has flattened out as if troweled—a billiard table landscape. And further west, halfway to Elkhart, the land tosses and turns like an insomniac. It is all Kansas and it is never dull.

We have seen several ring-necked pheasants by the side of the road. They don't seem to be frightened by the traffic and I suppose they're safe from hunters until fall.

We pulled into Elkhart at twenty minutes after five. Brooks Littrell told me that Velma Roberts owns the El Rancho Motel, where we are staying, and the restaurant building next door. She also owns the Elkhart Motel a few blocks away and its restaurant. Plus she owns almost all the apartment houses in Elkhart and several rental houses. Where did she get her money? She earned it, starting from virtually nothing.

Monday, April 18, 1988

It had rained on us much of the way into Elkhart Sunday afternoon, and before dawn I looked out the window of our little palace and saw the streetlights reflected in the pavement. If it wasn't raining, it certainly was damp. And chilly. The heavy shirt and winter coat felt good as we made our way to the restaurant. Brooks Littrell was waiting for us, ready to lend his big Suburban to the cause, as he had done before.

We find it is better to assemble in one car, if possible, in our search for the trail, because it eliminates the need for radio communication, which is sporadic at best. But not many people have vehicles large enough for all of us— certainly a Suburban is more comfortable than the back of a pickup truck.

As we drove to Boise City, the sky lightened and the clouds seemed to roll back. By the time we arrived in that Panhandle town, the sun was shining. The cold front had passed.

On the square we met Jere and some others. There was Bill Wheatley, from Clayton, New Mexico, a former state senator and strong friend of the trail, probably in his upper eighties. David Hutchison, whose ranch is nearby the Burdick Ranch, and who hoped to get us in the Burdick spread to see Camp Nichols. Unfortunately, Burdick was adamant—no admission, period. The ranch goes on the auction block at two tomorrow afternoon. We shall try to return someday after the hammer falls. David is fighting a heavy cold, but still is extraordinarily friendly and seems to be pleased to be able to help us.

Louise Dawson was there, an extremely pleasant, savvy woman, who lives on the Kenton road, northwest of Boise City. Louise is a member of the local historical society. She and her husband managed the Burdick place for ten years. Their present place is also next door to the Burdick ranch.

Brooks Littrell, left, and Dan and Carol Sharp.

Louise is still recovering from cataract surgery. On our last trip to western Kansas, she was in the hospital, but she wanted to get up and join us anyway.

Next we met Dan and Carol Sharp, who own the 11,000-acre ranch next to the Gorman Ranch, which is owned by Dan's father. Dan is forty-two and looks thirty-two, a slender guy with a mustache, wideset eyes with a crinkly smile. Leo thinks he looks like Burt Reynolds; I think he is better looking. Carol is also of slight build, and has piercing eyes: intense and pleasant.

Jeff Wells is also with us—he works with the soil conservation agency—as is his wife, Joann. Jeff is another wiry guy with a considerable stubble today. The summer sun is tough on his skin, so he grows a beard each year in self-defense.

Ralph Compton and his Beechcraft

We drove to the Boise City airport. It's a jumble of cor-
rugated iron buildings and a single asphalt landing strip.
A "ready room" holds a few worn-out chairs and some
folding tables. There's one john and we lined up patiently.
The pay telephone didn't work. Water and sandy mud from
the previous night's soaker were everywhere, inside and outside the building.

A hangar door opened and there sat a Mooney, built like
a baby P-51. Someone rolled out a Beechcraft. Together we
could seat six passengers. At last count there were a dozen
of us. Someone drove to town to find another pilot; he
showed up an hour later and rolled out a Piper Cherokee,
a six-place plane.

David Hutchison and the three pilots huddled over the
local aeronautical charts, while he explained where he

wanted us to go. I got assigned to the Beechcraft with Ralph Compton as pilot.

The Mooney started smoothly, moved a few yards from the ramp to the end of the runway and was airborne in seconds. Our Beech followed, and then the Piper. The Mooney was a speck ahead of us, a graceful little bird mixed in with the earth patterns as it hung below our horizon. Occasionally, as we banked, we could catch a glimpse of the big Piper following us. It looked strange—the gear doesn't retract.

We flew over the Sharp Ranch and once again saw that beautiful formation known as Autograph Rock; then over Dan's father's place, where rock cliffs have also been carved, with earlier dates. I could see the puddles that marked the site of Cold Spring.

Then on to the dramatic Flag Springs. From there we proceeded west; Rabbit Ears was on the horizon. Ralph zoomed down over the troubled Burdick ranch and Camp Nichols. What sad days these must be for Burdick. Some ranchers can make it, some can't. The line between them is exceedingly fine. The stakes are high; the gamble runs into the millions of dollars.

We needed to lose altitude in a hurry for some reason. Ralph must have felt he was in a fighter plane, for he rolled the little Beech over on one wing, headed down rapidly, and pulled out. That old ''g'' feeling I hadn't experienced since 1944 came back and for a few seconds my weight doubled. It was nowhere near the g-forces I had felt so often in my youth—there were times then when I blacked out as the blood was forced from my brain—but it was unpleasant nevertheless.

Aerial view of Camp Nichols

We had gone into New Mexico to photograph McNees Crossing, far to the west of the other planes, so we were the last to land.

Before we moved out to take in the sights on the ground which we had seen from the air, we had a surprise lunch in the ready room—a loaf of bread, two packs of cold cuts, hot coffee, cold drinks, potato chips, and cookies.

This handful of local trail trackers is so happy to find at last some national recognition coming their way. They had been studying the trail and watching the historic sites for years—in Wheatley's case, decades—with practically no company. They knew it was of vital importance to the development of the United States, yet, no one else seemed to care.

For years a growing group of us exchanged letters and

phone calls about preserving the trail. At last in the mid-1980s the pieces started to come together. Tired of the endless talk, I decided to act. Late one night in January 1985 I started to write a bill. Several hours later, my office floor was covered with notes, drafts, copies of other bills, and tons of supporting material. A bill emerged that looked good, and, with a few changes, it passed.

First I had to make two trips to Washington to make sure the right people—especially Senator Nancy Kassebaum of Kansas and Representative Bill Richardson of Santa Fe— had everything they needed to get it through. Representatives from the National Park Service spoke in favor of the bill. Ranch spokesman Dan Kipp made a strong case for respecting ranchers' rights. I agreed with him and strongly oppose giving the federal government the right to condemn land, and then take it over, simply because it is historically significant. Ninety-nine percent of the landowners along the trail will cooperate with the NPS, but one hundred percent stand opposed to the threat of condemnation.

In 1987 the Santa Fe Trail became a National Historic Trail, by Act of Congress. And now the efforts of that legion of local devotees are being rewarded. They see the prestigious National Park Service in their hometown, leading the way in an energetic study which will establish the importance of that historic highway in the national consciousness once and for all. How sweet it is for them. And for me.

We headed north out of Boise City, up toward Wolf Mountain. Following Jeff's pickup, we turned in at Bob Gayler's ranch. He owns some of the land we wanted to survey. Not home. On to the north. At a roadside park we found the ruts of the trail coming in from the right. But the pickup we were following seemed to have disappeared. Since we were still searching for the Aubry Route, we headed up into Colorado. But then we doubled back, concerned about our lead pickup.

As we headed south, one of our sharp-eyed passengers saw the long-bed pickup parked in a farmyard. We drove in. Jeff had decided to check with Helen Parker, Bob Gayler's sister. She had already called around and found Bob. He was on his way. He had forgotten that he had agreed to help us this morning.

As soon as he arrived, we headed back into Colorado to try to find more evidence of the Aubry Road. We found the little stone building where we had been with Leon Hollenback the week before. But no more ruts. The ground had all been worked. Back to Oklahoma.

Wandering through the hills near the Colorado-Oklahoma border, on or near the trail, we came upon the stone corral we had seen from the air. The ruts there lie to the south-southwest.

We headed south to the Strong Ranch and wound our way to the west, over some primitive two-track roads. Sometimes there was no road at all. Bob Gayler and Jeff Wells didn't hesitate; they knew where we were going. For miles there was no sign of that dramatic rock formation, Flag Springs. How is it that we saw the site so distinctly from the air and it is nowhere to be seen from the ground? We headed up through a draw between two low hills, looping around to the right. Rock piles were ahead of us on the horizon. As we drew closer it was obvious we were nearing that jumble of flagstones called Flag Springs.

What a gorgeous site! I picked my way over the mounds of flagstone and in a clearing there is a concrete building—or what remains of one. No roof, windows, or doors. It had a fireplace at one time. Snap ties are still in place. When was it built? I would say in the 1920s. Why was it built? Who knows? But it is an idyllic place, a good spot to escape from the pressures of the world. I moved around the lagoon formed by the spring to the pasture land, then up the opposite side, climbing a large hill to gain an overview of the place. From there I could see that the pool of water had collected behind an earthen dam.

After a few minutes to enjoy the place, we turned back to Boise City and the Sharp Ranch. We followed the ranch roads to a ranchhouse. Behind it is the sheer Autograph Rock.

Dan explained why they bought the place. "We knew we had to make a living," he said. "That was the first criterion in the selection of a ranch. This place met that requirement all right. But I wanted something more than that. I wanted a place that has a raw beauty to it, and more important than anything else, an aura of history. That's why we're here. Carol and I have never regretted it, not once. I still get a thrill walking under this outcrop, looking at these names cut in here more than a century ago."

I wish that every history teacher in the United States could spend an hour with Dan and Carol Sharp. They would learn something that no books could teach them.

"I want to show you something else," Dan said. We followed behind his pickup, out across the fields, heading for his father's ranch, "next door." Actually, it is about three miles away, or twenty minutes. A person can cut through the fields, as we did, or go by the hard-surfaced road. Either way, it is about the same time from one place to the other.

We arrived at another handsome ranch house. This one was backed by a much lower wall of rock. These inscriptions were older—some back to the early 1840s. I heard that there were a few from the late 1830s, but couldn't find them. Lots of forty-niners bound for California's El Dorado had left their marks. I wondered how many had met the fate of my great-grandfather, Dr. William Hugh Stephen Henderson: dead at the age of thirty-two, felled in the goldfields of tuberculosis.

Below the rock were two ancient stone buildings. Dan had heard that there was a stage station here once, and these were part of that complex of buildings. The roof on one was almost gone. The smaller one served as a springhouse, and from it flowed the Cold Spring referred to in the diaries of early teamsters. By then the sunlight was almost gone.

Tuesday, April 19, 1988

Mapping the trail in New Mexico is going to be fun, except for the maps we have. They cover a full county per map and some of these counties are very big. Hence, the maps are often the size of bed sheets. The section numbers are rarely marked in the squares, meaning I have to count them out and pencil them in, when transcribing the trail from old maps which do have the sections numbered. Often there are no section lines at all, which means I have to draw them in. However, I have no way of knowing where the surveyors' corrections fall, so I am apt to be off a mile or

The Rabbit Ears

more over a six-township block. Why can't the New Mexico cartographers do the same caliber job as those of other states?

After breakfast in Clayton, we were joined again by Bill Wheatley. We learned that Bill had lost his wife after a prolonged illness only last month. He is trying hard to make the adjustment, but I know it's rough. At least he has lots of friends around here. Everybody knows Bill and holds him in high regard.

He led us north toward McNees Crossing. On our left were the familiar Rabbit Ears. I remember the first time I saw them I wondered what the guy who named them was thinking of. I couldn't see anything resembling a rabbit. Then I learned that the two mounds were named for an Indian chief by that name.

Moving over the hill to come down to the McNees Crossing, I saw a group of cars and trucks parked ahead. Well, whadaya know, a reception committee. Upon coming closer I noticed that only one person was "one of us"—David Hutchison. The rest were the seven men needed to mount and paint a New Mexico historical marker for the crossing.

We turned into the field and stopped just a half mile ahead. There was a tall white marble marker on the right. I walked ahead and came down to a shelf of solid rock. The water was so shallow Leo was able to pick his way across without getting in over his shoe tops. There in the rock beneath my feet were two grooves. Could they be wagon tracks? Leo says yes; Bonita says no. I don't know, but I think they are. (Marc Simmons later said a person had to have a lively imagination to think that they were.)

We were joined in the field by Sue Richardson, head of the Union County Historical Society. She exemplifies the type of person who make the national efforts work. Without people like Sue the rest of us would be spinning our wheels. Paul Bentrup visited the office of the Clayton Chamber of Commerce about a year ago and noticed dozens of different brochures out on the counter. "Nothing here about the Santa Fe Trail," he groused. "Your historical society people ought to do something about that!"

So Sue did. She had a little piece printed at the newspaper office, and it is now out on the counter with the rest of the material.

On to the southwest we went with Bill Wheatley leading the way. The radios were working most of the time. We turned right and left, following the course of the trail. Turning left down the shaft of a T, I looked ahead and to the

Sue Richardson, left, Leo and Bonita Oliva, and the sign erected at McNees Crossing.

right. The trail should have been there, heading to our left and coming southward to intersect our road ahead nearly a mile. Wow! There in that unbroken pasture were three of the sharpest rut swales I had ever seen. Perfect.

At the top of the hill we stopped for pictures. David used his cowboy boots to kick out a round metal object from the gravel road, right where the trail crossed. "Hey, look!" he said. "A water pump from a Murphy wagon!"

Clearing the next rise, Wheatley stopped the caravan. There on the horizon, through nearly 180 degrees, were the landforms which guided the traders. To our left, the famous Rabbit Ears. Slightly to the right, the nondescript form of Mount Dora. Further to the right, the shallow peak of Round Mound, known today as Mount Clayton. Across the road and to the right, the peak of Sierra Grande, snowcapped yesterday but dry today. Then farther to our right, the scooped-out cone of the volcano, Mount Capulin. All had been sketched in the 1820s by Joseph C. Brown, surgeon for the Sibley expedition.

We moved quickly through the section line road network and wound down to the rock bed of a creek, then back up to the high ground again. That was Turkey Creek; we were searching for the Turkey Creek Camp. To the left was the stone corral we had seen from the air yesterday morning. We doubled back to the creek and turned right on the north bank onto a two-track. Stopping on a knoll, Bill read passages from Kate Gregg's book describing the 1825 Brown field notes.

Back in the cars, Jere poked to the east and we followed. The corral, according to Bill, was not trail related. Actually, it was a sheep corral, part of the enormous Eklund Ranch which extended far into Colorado. We stayed on the two-track for about a mile to the east, where we were forced to turn. Jere got out to look over the land. I turned right and kept moving out on the high ground above the creek bed. It was Leo who spotted some wagon tracks leading up out of the creek bed from the left; that would be where the wagons went down, but where did they come out?

I left the two-track, driving the Chrysler through the sage to higher ground. There was a depression of some sort there, but I couldn't tell where it came from or where it was going. Was it the trail?

Krakow was on the far bank. Leo got out and hollered over the chasm: "You have it over there, Jere. Are we in it over here?"

"I think so," Jere shouted back. "You're in one of several braided swales, headed down to this smooth rock crossing where I crossed the creek. I think you have it."

I checked the lines on my county highway map, the trail was right on Hobart Stocking's route. We had found the Turkey Creek Crossing of the Santa Fe Trail.

After lunch and a short rest we went on to the west, with Bill Wheatley again in the lead. We were approaching the ranch of the most remarkable woman I had met along the trail to date, Imogene Thoma. She owns a massive cattle ranch, some 13,000 acres and about 1,000 head of cattle, and farms it alone. Leo estimated that the spread is worth a great deal. We stopped at the ranch; Bill Wheatley had called earlier for permission to see the ruts and to try to find Rabbit Ears Campground.

A red pickup came around the corner of the barn. Imogene was driving it. There were three bales of hay on the back. She asked us to follow her, and she led us through the fields about two miles north of her house. We passed through the gates, Jere opening and closing them, as we neared Rabbit Ears Creek. The cattle recognized the pickup; Imogene feeds them every day from it. They were lowing and following as fast as their fat little legs would carry them.

As soon as we stopped they crowded around, hoping to get a handout. Leo was able to count a couple hundred of them before they bunched together; "I think that was about half," he said.

We came over a knob and there before us, next to the live water of Rabbit Ears Creek, was a dish-shaped meadow. We thought this had to be the camp. We could

Imogene Thoma's cattle, in search of a free meal.

verify it by going up the hill to catch the trail coming down.

"I think it will be a lot easier if you all go in the pickup," Imogene said. "One of you folks drive and I'll stay here."

Krakow got behind the wheel, and Leo, Bonita, Betty, Bill, the baled hay, and I jolted over the unbroken prairie to the high ground. There were four or five fine, gentle swales, right where Stocking said the trail ought to be. The cattle wouldn't leave us alone. They closed in on the tailgate, sniffing the hay.

We returned to Imogene and chatted about the trail for perhaps fifteen more minutes. "Hey, GIT!" she shouted to the cows, who had become bold enough to start pulling the bales over the tailgate. The cattle scattered.

"There are a bunch of rocks up there near the hill," she

said. "I have heard it said that there was a stage station up there but I haven't been able to prove it. Maybe someday some people who know what they're doing can poke around in there and find out for sure." Maybe so, but if they do, I hope there is a professional archaeologist among them. There have been entirely too many amateurs digging up artifacts from the historic trails, destroying evidence as they pull the junk from the earth.

We headed west to the overlook north of Round Mound and parked. I walked up on the embankment of the Santa Fe tracks, which converged toward Sierra Grande to the west. Cumulus clouds scudded overhead now and then; I had to wait five minutes to get a good shot of Round Mound. It was worth it.

The Eklund family, who owned one of the largest ranches in the West, was headquartered in Clayton. At the height of their power they built the Eklund Hotel there, which still stands. It isn't a hotel any longer, but the saloon and dining areas have been remodeled to capture the flavor of nineteenth century opulence. The main dining room is closed on Tuesdays, so Bill Wheatley made a telephone call and we had the whole room to ourselves for an elegant dinner.

Wednesday, April 20, 1988

We were nearing the end of the Cimarron Cutoff; I could almost see Santa Fe up ahead. We left Clayton for a long drive over to Colfax County and headed up to the New Mexico Point of Rocks. Jere knocked on the door of the handsome stone house situated beneath the towering pile

New Mexico's Point of Rocks

of rocks—the last (or first) of four Point of Rocks landmarks which served as landmarks for the teamsters.

A tall, kindly woman, Faye Gaines, greeted us. She told us that this spread was part of a ranch inherited by her husband, Garrett (Pete) Gaines, from his father. His grandfather had acquired the land in the latter part of the nineteenth century. She volunteered to show us the graves at the place.

We walked out in the fields to the east. After only a few steps a sharp, telltale rattle was heard. Bonita suddenly leaped into the air. She had barely missed stepping on a rattler, with perhaps an inch of rattles on his tail, coiled and ready to strike. As soon as she jumped back, the snake uncoiled and slithered down its hole.

"Oh, I wish we could have killed him," Faye said. "I

Grave of Isaac Allen

thought we had gotten them all but I guess you never do.''

We continued on to a mound of six or eight flagstones. Faye said, ''The headstone was broken when some guy from Las Vegas was caught digging in here. He was supposed to be some sort of Santa Fe Trail expert, but he never came back. He's dead now. Anyway, he broke the stone and we turned it face down to protect the inscription.''

I upended it. It contained the words:

Isaac Allen

1848

Nothing else. Faye thought the man was a trader, a victim of Indians, but said that was only hearsay.

She volunteered to show us the great spring gushing from

the face of the rock, so welcomed by the traders. We went up the gentle slope to a circular concrete cap resembling a cistern lid. "The spring is in there," she said, "and it is the source of the water supply for our house." She and Pete built that rock house themselves and have lived in it since the 1940s.

"Want to see the other graves?" she asked. Of course we did. "Just drive through that gate over there, I'll join you on the buggy."

We moved through the gate and heard a roar from the garage. Out popped a red Yamaha four-wheel off-road vehicle. She sailed over the pasture and I tried to keep up in the Chrysler without turning everybody into a milkshake. She pulled up to a red pickup; that must be Pete. She was explaining who we were, I supposed. Pete drove over and asked if we wanted to ride in the back. We did. But I didn't get the word and the truck went on without me.

"Hop aboard," said Faye. I jumped on the Yamaha and away we went. Faye led the way to another grave, about 500 yards from the house. It was covered with several flagstones and a gnarly bush was growing from its center. Then on to two more, perfectly aligned, almost identical graves. In all we visited eight more. Faye said she had heard that two or three men had been killed by Indians at first. When Mexican traders stumbled onto the site of the carnage a day or so later, they, too, were killed by Lo. A later caravan arrived after the Indians had left and found the bodies badly damaged by wolves. They buried them where they were found. The Gaines family has been able to learn nothing more.

Pete drove us out in the fields among the dozens of tipi

Jere Krakow, Faye Gaines, and her buggy

rings left by the Indians. Then into Youngblood Canyon, where another spring was flowing freely.

"Old Charley Youngblood holed up in here," Pete explained. "He was the guy who trapped out the last of the lobo wolves. And the next canyon in is where Black Jack Ketchum hid out. You hear about him? He's the train robber. They shot and captured him and took him to Clayton for trial. First they had to get him well, and in order to do that they had to chop off his arm where he had been shot. Then after he was in good shape they hung him. Popped his head right off, they did. But he's kind of a folk hero today."

Later I had heard that Pete was one of the two ranchers who had opposed the SFT bill. He is not the rheumy-eyed old geezer I had suspected him to be, but a very nice fellow who couldn't do enough for us. Strange how a person's perception can change with familiarity.

Just west of the bridge over the Canadian River we stopped at a ranch on the south side of the highway. Jere drove in to meet the owners and we waited on the highway. It was a sunny, quiet day, and rarely did a car or truck pass on Highway 56. In the middle of a reverie, Jere radioed: "I'm coming back up the lane. This is the ranch-house for the Dos Rios Ranch, owned by Joe and Sue Knowles. They are going to take us to the Rock Crossing of the Canadian."

Another pickup truck. This one had barbed wire and trash in the back. We piled in and agreed to help unload the scrap at their dump. Joe abandoned a lucrative medical practice in Borger, Texas, because he wanted to raise Longhorns. He seems to be about fifty-five and has wideset eyes which glow with the excitement of life. He got so wrapped up in trail history that he tended to stammer.

The Knowleses took us to the old group of buildings down by the river. We crossed a first-class little bridge that Joe had built over the Cimarron River (the New Mexican one, not the Kansas one). A few dozen yards ahead it flows into the Canadian.

The Knowleses practice holistic ranching and are very careful about disturbing the ecology of their land. They don't drive in their pastures more than a couple of times a year, so they were doing something special for us. We followed the fence row out in the pasture about two miles and angled down to the river bluff.

There we could see the great gorge of the Canadian, and a gentle slope coming down from the mesas to the east.

The rock in the Canadian is hard sandstone, and the wagons would have crossed it easily. Jere did, by stepping from one rock to another. There was not only a rock bed, but smooth rock leading out of the stream for perhaps a dozen yards.

"When you stop to think about it," Joe said, "they could have crossed nowhere else but in this vicinity. There is deep sand all the way from here to the Colorado line. To the south the gorge is up to 100 feet deep for nearly 100 miles. When Marc Simmons was here we walked all the way back there to the end of my property, which happens to be the southeast corner of the Maxwell land grant. Marc pointed to that rock over there and said he bet that Kit Carson had sat on that rock, waiting for the traders to arrive so he could give them military protection to Santa Fe."

The ruts were right where they were supposed to be, climbing out of the Canadian.

I felt that we were really nearing civilization now. We took Interstate 25, headed south toward Santa Fe. We came to a rise in the highway and there, far away on the horizon, was the last of the great landmarks, Wagon Mound.

Thursday, April 21, 1988

Jere had called ahead for reservations at the historic Plaza Hotel in Las Vegas; we were really looking forward to that. We had stayed there a couple of months earlier; big rooms, high ceilings, fine restaurant—a truly great experience. Last night was just the opposite. We were on the third floor, in a closed hallway. The temperature was eighty-three degrees in our room, warmer in the hall. Outside it was

Fort Union, outlined against a cloudy sky

in the fifties, but there was no way to get the cool air in. I complained and finally got a fan. The room was one of the smallest we'd had and poorly lit. Never again, Plaza.

Early this morning we drove to the road to Fort Union, where we met a woman I had been wanting to meet for a long time, Melody Webb, historian for the Santa Fe office of the NPS. With her was Neil Mangum, recently of the Custer Battlefield National Monument, and Douglas C. McChristian, superintendent at Fort Union.

We looked at those great ruts along the road leading to the fort. A couple of miles in we could see the Cimarron Cutoff twisting off a knoll and down to the flat area beside the road. Coming in from the left was the Mountain Branch. They met right in front of us.

We drove to the Sapello Stage Station, which is in use today as a ranchhouse. It's the original structure, except for the addition of a long front porch. The ruts come near the place, heading toward an easy crossing of Sapello Creek.

Beyond the station was Fort Union's stone corral, where cattle were fattened for use by the troops. After we looked it over, we went back to the highway and took the gravel road into Tiptonville. The old store building there, of frame and stone, is still being used in the ranch complex.

On the east side of I-25 we traveled north toward the old Watrous store, crossing the bridge over Mora Creek. A few yards to the south, the Sapello Creek flows in.

When we pulled into the yard of the Watrous store, now the Doolittle Ranch, I was unprepared for what I saw. We were greeted by gorgeous Nicole King, the daughter-in-law of Barbara Doolittle. She is from Holland, a former exchange student who once stayed at the ranch. And then Barbara herself, a charming, gracious woman who welcomed us warmly.

She was concerned—one of their calves was sick. It had wandered to a hiding place and couldn't be found, despite a two-day search. Nevertheless, Barbara took time to show us around.

This ranchhouse was once the old Watrous store and was built of adobe. It was large then, but neither well maintained nor attractive. Barbara and the late Jim Doolittle bought the site for their ranching operation, along with 13,000 acres. The rear building had been demolished, so Barbara had another constructed to close in the landscaped courtyard. It is elegant and offers everything that a human being could want by way of habitation. Barbara Doolittle has superb taste and the means to interpret it successfully.

I mused aloud on how wonderful it would be to set up a computer in the corner of the natatorium and write books in my bathing suit while the blizzards raged outside. We found that we had a mutual friend in St. Louis in one of those "small world" discoveries—Pris (Mrs. Sanford) McDonnell.

I had a question for Barbara: "Will you adopt me?" She had one for me: "Can you find a sick calf?"

In Las Vegas we had lunch and I made a quick trip to Los Artesanos Bookshop to meet the owners, old customers of ours. They had heard we were publishing the Brown book and urged me to consider reprinting *Peter and Brownie Follow the Trace*. We will, someday.

We picked up Joe Herrera, who was born and raised in Tecolote, just to the south of Las Vegas. Joe proved to be a marvelous escort, taking us on the service roads and out into the boonies, where we saw the trail ruts on either side of our path. We toured Tecolote, the town where Marian and Richard Russell had their first store, which was bulldozed in the 1930s, as I understand it. Then on to San Miguel and that haunting Catholic church. The wind was screeching now, but I got out of the car, braving the blowing sand, and went into the courtyard. In front was the grave of one of the priests from the nineteenth century. It was decorated with a rosary fashioned by the hands of loving parishioners. The cross was formed of welded railroad spikes, the beads from nipples of galvanized pipe. In back of the church are the headstones of perhaps two dozen people, almost all of whom died in the nineteenth century.

We drove the back roads to San Jose. The trail, the interstate highway, and the railroad were all following the "fishhook"—that pathway which loops to the south before heading northwest to enter the City of Holy Faith.

San Jose del Vado

Friday, April 22, 1988

Marc Simmons and Bill deBuys of the Nature Conservancy knocked on the door of our motel room about eight. I had met Bill in Boise City at the Pizza Hut the night before he was to bid on the Burdick Ranch, and I was eager to hear his report. He told us it sold to a fellow from Texas at $128 an acre. Nearly $2 million changed hands. The new owner is expected to send one of his sons to Oklahoma to run it. Bill had dropped out of the bidding at $115 an acre.

"After the Texas guy had bought the place, I approached him to find out his attitude on selling for the site of Camp Nichols and some of the trail ruts," Bill said. "He was pretty cagey. 'You know,' he told me, 'you are asking me to sell the best grass on the place.' That's not true, of course, but it tells me we may have trouble getting Camp Nichols. Maybe we can at least gain access to it, with permission."

That's a lot more than we got with Burdick.

It was good to see Marc again. He came in with just one aluminum crutch. I greeted him at the door: "Throw away that crutch; you're cured!"

"Hey, thanks."

I couldn't help but think back to the day I first met Marc. It was on the lawn of the Bingham-Waggoner House in Independence, during the first OCTA convention in 1983. And I remembered how shy he had been when I brought him to Washington a couple of years later, to help lobby for the Santa Fe Trail bill. He would wait out in the hall while we lobbied the congressional people. He was whole then, before that awful head-on collision which almost took his life eighteen months ago. But he's coming back, and someday he'll be his old self again.

Marc is far and away the most intense scholar the Santa Fe Trail has ever known. His library has 10,000 volumes and grows daily. It is housed in a separate building in his compound.

But that isn't what makes Marc Simmons great. He is great because he shares what he has. If he doesn't know the answer to a question, he will hunt until he can come up with one. He is kindness personified.

We piled into two cars, Marc and Bill riding with Jere, and Leo and Bonita with Betty and me. The cantankerous NPS radios connected us, sometimes.

As we approached I-25 we heard the first message from Marc. "See this subdivision over here on the left? They are adding to it now, and getting dangerously close to the ruts of the Santa Fe Trail."

We drove to the location of the old Kozlowski's Ranch, where the headquarters of the Forked Lightning Ranch are located. "I think the future of the Forked Lightning is cloudy," Marc said. "E. E. Fogelson died, and evidently there are problems with the estate."

That would be bad news. Fogelson and his wife, actress Greer Garson, saved the Pecos ruin almost alone and funded the marvelous interpretive center there manned by the National Park Service. They have been good, sensitive neighbors to the trail.

As we drove to the Forked Lightning, we looked off to the left of the interstate and caught a good view of the Pecos ruins, the site of an early civilization in what had been wilderness.

Marc got his first look at the new wing of the Pecos National Monument interpretive center, which I suppose was funded by the Fogelson estate, as the main building had been.

We passed through the old town of Pecos; again, picturesque squalor greeted us on all sides. Someday I hope to have the time to photograph this latter-day ruin.

Now began a driving odyssey with Marc crackling directions and giving us historical background over the radios, which worked most of the time. We drove back and fourth around I-25, catching glimpses of ruts along the way. Usually they were close to the service roads, sometimes they were far back in the hills.

Marc directed us to the Pigeon Ranch, where only one modern-looking building survives. The decisive Battle of Glorieta Pass transpired here. We looked up at a rock high over us. A young sharpshooter was ordered up there, said Marc, but he complained to his general that he had had a dream the night before that he would be killed in battle this day.

"Nonsense," said the general, "we all have such dreams before battles. Get up there and do your job."

The youngster did, promptly drawing a ball between the eyes.

We went a little farther and stopped, crossed the service road, and headed through an open gate down a draw in Apache Canyon. Partway down we turned to the left and soon came into view of an ancient bridge across the canyon.

"This bridge was originally built in the 1850s," Simmons said. "And it figured significantly during the Battle of Glorieta Pass. I call this the Battle of Apache Canyon, which was a prelude to the main battle two days later. The confederates retreated over this bridge, toward us, and when the last of them came over they chopped out the bridge floor. The Union troops saw what had happened, but concluded that their mounts could jump the gorge. One by one, they did, and all made it but one.''

Both approaches to the bridge are now washed out. The wood deck is in bad shape; it probably has been replaced at least twice since the battle. But the foundation rocks remain the same.

We came to the site of Johnson's Ranch. It is next to a quaint, box-like Catholic church with many crosses in the graveyard. The Johnson site is virtually a vacant lot; there is nothing at all where the main ranch building used to be.

The land has changed greatly as we've moved west. Now it is heavily forested, mostly with coniferous trees. It resembles a mountain landscape, yet we aren't quite in the mountains. It is a relaxed land, cool and peaceful today.

Marc directed us to vistas of ruts along the service roads. We came to a fairly new golf course high above Santa Fe, probably about the same place where Gregg's artist stood when he painted the scene of the jubilant traders rolling into Santa Fe. The city is spread out below us like a jewel; it is a breathtaking view. The ruts here were recently plowed up in the development of the golf course. A corner of one cuts though the undeveloped land, then goes back though the chain link fence to disappear in a fairway.

On Vieja Rostro we passed the Santa Fe home of Georgia O'Keeffe. Then we went to the National Cemetery, where Gov. Charles Bent had the honor of being the first occupant. William Bent's brother, he was sent from Bent's Old

Mounds of earth, which were once Fort Marcy, overlook Santa Fe.

Fort to become governor of the New Mexico territory right after it had been won by the United States. He set up shop in Taos.

But Mexicans and some Indians were displeased with the sellout of Mexican governor Manuel Armijo, who abandoned New Mexico to Stephen Watts Kearny without a shot being fired. The Taos Revolt ensued, and one of the first casualties was Charles Bent. He was lying mortally wounded, pierced with arrows, when one vicious Indian twisted his bowstring around his head, just above the ears, and deftly popped off his scalp.

The amazing Francis X. Aubry lies in the next cemetery to the south. Someone lost track of things, and his stone is missing. We now have no idea which grave is his.

We went up to the bluff overlooking Santa Fe, where

Fort Marcy was built right after the Mexican War. There are condominiums and apartment buildings up there now, but some mounds of earth out on the point overlooking the city mark the remains of the old fort. Many a soldier spent many a lonely night on guard duty up here, serenaded by the wind, and sometimes the snow, sleet, and rain. Now nothing but those silent mounds of earth is left. Not even (today at least) the wind.

There was another stop to make—Burro Alley. This is a block-long street quite near the plaza, a lane which once bordered a number of small corrals housing thousands of donkeys between their trips on the trails. They might go to Missouri, or they might go to Chihuahua. Marc described how a century ago Charles Lummis said that Santa Fe should erect a statue to the burro. The city is just now getting around to it.

As we drove back across the Oklahoma panhandle, darkness came upon us. The sky was clear, stars bright. Venus was close to the moon. The lights of Elkhart came up ahead and we pulled into the El Rancho.

Saturday, April 23, 1988

I opened the door of our motel room at 7:15 and saw the Oliva rig. Sometime during the night they had parked right next to our Chrysler. There may be a romance going between those vehicles, but before they have my blessing that motor home is going to have to bathe.

This is our last day of trail tracking this trip. We have two people to contact—Ron French, our old pal from Ulysses, and Lester Unruh of Copeland. We know that virtually all of the Middle Crossing trail between Cimarron and Wagon Bed Springs has been lost to farming, but we have to get what we can get.

We headed to the northeast on U.S. 56. At Sublette we examined the 1939 aerials at the county historical museum in the old depot. The traces were visible virtually all the way across the county. Leo and I checked my maps against the photographic evidence and found the lines matched almost perfectly. That is good news.

We pulled into the Dermot elevator, where Leo had arranged to meet Ron French. Ron is a recent devotee to the trail, converted by his schoolteacher wife, Karla.

Leo and Bonita piled into Ron's pickup and we drove to the ranch of Gerald Schmidt, where Ron led us out into the pasture near the house.

"The ruts are right in here," he said.

Only by using a strong imagination and backing off some distance could we discern any evidence of the old wagon passage. If the ruts had been any fainter they would have been invisible.

A burly man of about sixty-five approached us. He was dressed in bib overalls and his face had a leathery look; he had spent many years in this Kansas sun.

Gerald Schmidt knew practically nothing about the trail, but he brought with him an aerial photo-map provided to him by the Soil Conservation Service.

"Maybe this will help you folks," he said, unrolling the big photo on the hood of the car. It was a picture of his ranch, and it covered practically the whole hood.

"Good gosh!" I exclaimed, "How much land do you have here?"

"Oh, quite a bit," he said modestly. Silence. Then, "Eleven, twelve, thirteen thousand acres, somewhere in there."

The traces from those photos, taken more than a dozen years ago, confirmed where we thought the trail was, but we couldn't see it from the ground in either direction.

"Do you want to see it from the air?" Schmidt asked. At the end of the lane was a six-place Cessna. "I'll be glad to take you up but I don't know that I could tell you where the trail is."

Darn! We didn't have enough time. I would love to go up with him, but it was impossible to do that and get to Larned by six. We had to turn him down.

Two boys were playing in the yard with the dogs. "Are those yours?" I asked.

"My grandkids," he responded.

"Do they know how lucky they are?"

"Nope."

That seemed to draw him out. "They are here more than they are at their own home, which is fine by me. They drive that four-wheel buggy. They go for airplane rides with me. We have a summer place up in Salida, Colorado, and I fly up there with them in an hour and a half. We keep a car and a 4x4 pickup there at the airport. It's only a few minutes from a ski slope, and the boys enjoy doing all that with us."

We continued studying the aerial photo for signs of rut traces. Schmidt's hand glided over the map. It was gnarled and weatherbeaten, the skin scarred and tough as leather. Those hands had seen a lifetime of work, but now the man was obviously enjoying this life he had made for himself.

Lester Unruh helps Leo Oliva through his fence.

We took Ron back to the grain elevator and left for Copeland and a visit with Lester Unruh. We found him at home on his big ranch north of town. He was helping his father fix some farm machinery. Lester is a tall, good looking guy in his mid-thirties. He and his father are grain farmers and have invested a fortune in their own private grain elevator. The spread obviously was prosperous.

Leo and Bonita got in Lester's pickup and we drove several miles northwest.

"This is about the only pasture we have which isn't broken out," Lester said. "Yet, the ruts seem to be getting shallower and shallower."

Well, I guess so. I couldn't see them at all. I walked back and forth over them, got my eye close to the ground, and did every trick I could but I couldn't see a thing. Lester admitted he couldn't see them either, today. Maybe, he thought, we could stop by when the grama grass was a little more mature, and then perhaps we could see some traces.

An irrigation ditch snaked through the property along the bed of an old creek. On the other side prairie dogs stood on their haunches and barked at us. Ground squirrels scurried across our path as we walked back to the cars.

Our next destination offered more excitement. Shortly after our last trip ended Leo had received a package from Noel Ary of the Kansas Heritage Center in Dodge City. It contained a newspaper article written in 1969 about something we had never heard of before—the Black Pool, northeast of Ford.

We hightailed it over the back roads to Ford and drove to the point where a little two-track left the main gravel

The Black Pool

road, just past the "Boot Alley" we had seen a couple of weeks ago. I pulled into the section. Leo and Bonita parked on the shoulder and got out. We waited for them to get into the Chrysler, but then I noticed that they were talking with a man in a blue pickup. He turned out to be Charles Hensley, the brother of the landowner. Leo charmed him into guiding us to the Black Pool.

Leo and Bonita got into his pickup and we followed, winding over the diminishing two-track to a rise in the rolling prairie, where we stopped short, got out, and looked into a strange, rock-lined hole in the prairie. The rocks seemed to dam up a nearly dry wash, and on top of the "dam" was an inscription. It was dated 1843 and seemed to be authentic. Dozens of other inscriptions had been cut into the Dakota sandstone formation, most of them from recent times. At the bottom was what appeared to be an algae-polluted puddle—the Black Pool.

The author of the article we have says he lowered a rock on all the line he had but couldn't find the bottom of the pool. Charles told us that he had heard of cowboys doing the same thing with their lariats. They couldn't find the bottom either.

We left the Black Pool convinced that we had uncovered something new for trail buffs and headed northwest over twenty miles of dusty gravel and pot-holed asphalt toward Larned.

After a quick cleanup at the Best Western, we headed west for Fort Larned, where the Kansas Corral of the Westerners was having their spring meeting and dinner of "authentic fort food." We were guests of Bonita and Leo. I felt sorry for the authentic soldiers.

A highlight of the night was the renewing of an acquaintance with Bill and Martha Chalfant, whom I had met in Hutchinson. I remember at the intermission of the SFTA banquet in Hutchinson, right after I had been given that embarrassing minute-long standing ovation, they hustled to their little supper club nearby where we had several drinks. There I met the remarkable Janet Lecompte of Colorado Springs, and David Gaines, the keynote speaker. We were regaled by the stories of Adrian Bustamante and David Sandoval. I was the dumbest guy there, a situation which I enjoy because I always learn something. But we had missed Sam Arnold, the celebrated Denver restaurateur, who had entertained the assemblage in the banquet hall with some numbers on his musical saw.

During my conversation with Chalfant I realized that he was the fellow who had worked so hard developing the route south from Fort Leavenworth through Topeka, the route that heretofore had escaped me. He had developed the trace through work at the National Archives. Thus, the one big hole in my studies had been filled.

George Elmore was there in full uniform. George had escorted us that fascinating day to Camp on Pawnee Fork, the new Fort Larned blockhouse, and the Hancock-Custer site. He gave us his splendid slide presentation on the restoration of the fort. I was so sleepy that I could barely stay awake; yet, the material was so engrossing I didn't dare go to sleep.

Sunday, April 24, 1988

This latest search for the Santa Fe Trail is now over, and all that remains is the exploration of the Mountain Branch. We packed our stuff into the Chrysler and left the Townsman after nearly four hours of clearing the tapes of field notes. Back to St. Louis.

IV. MAY 14-22, 1988

Saturday, May 14, 1988

Even though this was the beginning of the end, I had a strong feeling of elation as we headed west from St. Louis on Highway 40 this morning.

I had worked late last night in the office, much of the time devoted to translating lines from Stocking's maps, plus the USGS quads, to the Colorado and New Mexico highway maps. The Colorado maps are poorly reproduced but at least they are the normal scale of ½":1 mile. Not so those of New Mexico. They are little more than half that, and the type is so small as to be virtually unreadable, even with good reproduction. Whoever made the decision to do it that way certainly didn't have the user in mind. Furthermore, the enormous Maxwell tract evidently has never been surveyed. All we have to go by are parallels of latitude and meridians of longitude. What a mess!

Sunday, May 15, 1988

It was a crisp, sunshiny morning when we walked into the restaurant in Junction City for breakfast. When we walked out forty minutes later the sun was still shining, but the entire southeastern sky had turned to indigo; a stinker of a storm was on the way. We returned to the room and turned on the TV. The weather channel forecaster pointed out the heavy thunderstorms booming across our part of Kansas. We left hurriedly and got into the Chrysler just as the first drops started falling.

As we headed west at 72 MPH, large drops of rain propelled by a thirty-mile-an-hour wind crashed against the windshield at more than a hundred miles an hour. Life in a popcorn popper!

The rough, broken country around Junction City was now leveling out. Wheat which hadn't begun to sprout when our Santa Fe Trail adventure started was now nearly a foot high.

At noon we stopped in Oakley for lunch. We were making extraordinarily good time, so we decided to head south on 83 to visit the Chalk Pyramids mentioned on the Kansas road map. The country was flat prairie no more; in fact, it was beginning to resemble the Jornada. It reminded me of one of my trips through the West in the 1940s, when I caught my first astonished view of South Dakota's Badlands.

We watched our mileage carefully and at approximately the right place saw a crudely lettered sign advertising the Chalk Pyramids. It didn't tell us where to turn, so we kept going. Then we crossed the Smoky Hill River, and we could tell by one map that we had gone too far.

We could have doubled back, but I figured that the at-
traction couldn't have been very important or a decent sign
would have been on the highway. Anyway, the Cuartelejo
Pueblo ruins were just ahead on the right; we would see
them instead.

A highway sign directed us to the ruins off Highway 95.
And also to Lake Scott Park. We saw the lake and went
all the way to the point where 95 gets back on U.S. 83.
No sign and no indication of the ruins at all. So we filed
Cuartelejo in with the Chalk Pyramids. If they aren't worth
signing, they surely aren't worth seeing.

We continued into Colorado and hit Highway 50 west
of Lamar. We headed into Las Animas. After we had
unloaded our stuff at the motel, we drove into town. It's
a good-sized town, but the business district, like that of
Trinidad, has been hit by a depression. Half the places of
business seemed to have been abandoned.

When crossing the bridge, I noticed that the Arkansas
River presented a fairly typical view; a slight braiding,
twenty or thirty yards wide and only a few inches deep,
but a good strong flow. It was hard to believe that only
100 miles or so upstream it was rushing through the Royal
Gorge, a foaming cataract of whitewater.

Later I decided to get a good photograph of it. I parked
on the highway ramp, left the flashers on, and walked out
onto the bridge to shoot over the river and into the sun.
Spectacular! I packed up to go to the car and noticed one
of the knobs from my new tripod was missing. I also noticed
some red, blinking lights down behind my car. I took my
time walking back, looking for the knob and ignoring the

darned cop. Just before reaching the car, I saw the handle lying in the road. I put it back on, looked up, and the cop was gone. Lucky for him, for I was in no mood to humor a martinet.

After dinner we took a walk over the bridge across the Arkansas. A huge truck rolled over it and the bridge started galloping. It shook for a good twenty seconds after the truck had passed. But we kept going. A big yellow-billed magpie was digging for critters in the sand along the watercourse. Thousands of cliff swallows on their Spitfire wings raced through the swarms of gnats with open chops. Redwinged blackbirds flitted between the marsh grasses and the utility wires. We looked down into the river and saw two carp puckered up, sucking dessert out of the riverbed. I threw some pebbles their way and scared the hell out of them.

A priority of this trip was making a color photograph of Bent's Old Fort for the cover of Bill Brown's book. I had shot it at sunset, but since it faces east, the best shot would be at dawn. Sunrise in Denver, according to the *Post,* would come at 5:45. That would be about 5:30 here. So I'll set the alarm for 4:30, and we'll see what happens.

Monday, April 16, 1988

By the time I had finished dressing the sky was already getting light. I wondered if I could get to the fort thirteen miles away in time to shoot the sunrise. I headed west on Highway 194, alone, and don't think I met another car along the way. At 5:25 I could see the reddening of the horizon in the mirror. The sky changed from crimson to bright orange in the space of minutes. Birds by the thousands swarmed over the feedlots. All vehicles in the ranch yards were still at rest and the yard lights were still on.

Yesterday the car's air conditioner was on; this morning I punched the heat button. I looked over to the left, to the Arkansas River perhaps a mile away. Somewhere between us went the great caravans along the Mountain Branch of the Santa Fe Trail. The pulses of the traders would be quickening now, and I supposed their vigilance relaxed a little as they anticipated arrival at that great sentinel of the plains, Bent's Fort.

Heavily-laden wagons would be coming southwest from Independence and Westport and Fort Leavenworth, drawn by a dozen head of oxen. And coming the other way would be the lighter wagons, rich with furs and the silver of Taxco and Guadalajara. Some of each would be driven by Yankees, swearing in English; and Mexicans, swearing in Spanish.

Bands of lavender now appeared above the western horizon, as the cloud tops got their first peek at the sun of the sixteenth of May. I rounded a curve just 12.7 miles from U.S. 50 and there she was, out on the plain of the Arkansas, still shrouded in shadow but about to come alive. There was a single light in the parapets.

I parked the Chrysler at the first turnout and walked west to the main gate. It was locked to vehicular traffic, of course, since the fort doesn't open to the public until eight. I walked in anyway and began the long hike down the macadam pathway. The birds raised a cacophony; a shrill, constant chattering. They seemed oblivious to me. It was plain to see why they were so happy—the mosquitoes were big, juicy, and as voracious of me as the birds were of them.

We have one cover shot of Bent's Fort for the Brown book. Lisa liked the cart in the foreground but she didn't like the nearby woodpile. She asked me to shoot it without the wood. So I lined the wood up with the cart and fired away, both color and black-and-white. Then I circled out into the bottom, where the dead grasses of last summer were still matted down, trying to hold back the new grasses. Sunflower pods were still there, as they had been in my earlier picture, but I decided to let the entire bottom serve as a frame for the lower portion of the photograph only and not worry about the sides.

By this time the cart was out of the picture, but I caught a glint from a hubcap. A car was parked behind the fort. I moved to the right a little and it disappeared. I also saw a small, colorful farm wagon back there. I decided to go around to the south side later and see what kind of a foreground device this would make. First I circled through the matted grasses, back toward the road, shooting as I stalked the subject.

As I walked around the corner of the fort toward the wagon, I came upon a flock of fat Dominic chickens, including a very noisy rooster bent upon announcing the new day. They held still for a half-dozen shots. This is the breed which was at the fort in trail days. The staff had managed to find a supply of the rare chicks from an Iowa hatchery. I went around the front of the fort for more shooting. As I did, I saw a ranger raising the American flag on the cottonwood sapling used as a flagstaff. Then I had to do the whole job over again, as the flag really added something.

I headed back down the path to the car. I hoped. When I had begun shooting, I happened to look back to the car

A rooster and Dominic chickens greet the dawn at Bent's Old Fort.

and couldn't see it. I had parked it just below the old entrance, a rock archway which carries the words "Bent's Old Fort" in the cross span. Periodically, as I changed positions, I looked toward it. No Chrysler. I began to feel a considerable anxiety. Sure, I had insurance and I could rent a car, but damn, that would be a lot of trouble.

Now, as I walked from the fort to the road, it became more and more evident that the car had been stolen. I made the last curve, now only 100 yards from where I had parked it, and could still see nothing.

But suddenly I caught a glint of metal, and there it was, right where I had left it. Curiously, it was impossible to see from anywhere to the east.

Since we weren't scheduled to rendezvous until noon, Betty and I went for another walk down to the Arkansas

River. This time she brought her field glasses and we were able to get a better look at many of the birds. We left the bridge and walked down to the slough, but were thwarted by standing water and couldn't reach the main channel. We went back to the bridge deck and watched the big magpie fly to his nest and then on to a telephone wire to keep an eye on us. Far below, in a quiet backwater, thousands of minnows were socializing. The insects were thick in the air; the cliff swallows flew about us at great speed, picking off the bugs while somehow managing to miss each other.

At noon we met the team at the Cow Palace restaurant. It was a joy to see Jere, Leo, and Paul Bentrup again. (Bonita would come along later.) Ava and Tom Betz joined us. Tom is a third-generation newspaperman who owns *The Lamar Daily News*. Ava is the author of a fine commissioned history of Prowers County, a copy of which was given to me by Paul Bentrup. We also met the new team leader, John Paige, of Denver, and Don Hill, the superintendent at Bent's Fort. They would be with us all day.

After lunch we drove south and west out of town, into Bent County. We turned north at a wide spot in the road called Prowers. The name takes up as much space as the town does. There, while we waited for Paul Bentrup to catch up with us, we parked under a water tower large enough to take care of that town for the next century with one fill. Behind it was a row of rusting combines and other farm machinery.

Paul finally arrived—"Greetings and salutations!"— so we drove north over an ancient iron bridge, circled around to the left, drove through a field, and came to the site of Old Fort Lyon.

As usual, Paul came well prepared. He had photocopies of historic plats of the place. We noticed there were a number of low, flat-topped mounds in the field. They were the foundations of the buildings of the old fort. Using copies of the original ground plan, we were able to site them all, even the flag pole in the center of the parade ground.

The plat gave the direction and number of chains distant for the Santa Fe Trail. It came out to sixty paces north. I started pacing it off and came to an embankment, below which was a small irrigation ditch. I looked over to the north for about ten more yards. And, by golly, there they were! A number of swales headed in the right direction—due east and west. That really felt good! I kept on to the north, getting a shoeful of water as I misjudged the firmness of the brush by the creek.

Tom Betz had shown to me a picture he had taken of Bent's New Fort from a low-flying plane. The moat around the parapets was plainly in view. Now we would see it from the ground.

We drove back east of the iron bridge, through a wire gate, and up a rather steep hill. A utility pole was at the very top of the rise. "See that pole?" Tom asked.

"You bet," I said.

"That's right in the middle of the northeast bastion."

I took a bearing. It was 260 degrees. We moved to the top. A large marker overlooked the old iron bridge far below and to the west. The center of the U formed by the trenches was full of scattered rocks, more or less in rows—all that remains of Bent's New Fort. Here and there were fresh

Paul Bentrup, left, and Tom Betz inspect unauthorized excavations at Bent's New Fort.

diggings, the marks of an amateur archaeologist. Someone unauthorized had been excavating the site with a shovel. Tom promised to get the sheriff on the matter. That sort of thing had to stop.

We moved south toward the river and the headgate of the Amity Irrigation District. The rocks dropped abruptly into the reservoir. Down by the waterline, and completely inaccessible when the water is this high, are a number of petroglyphs. There are names and initials carved on the rocks atop the bench where we were, but all appeared to me to be from this century, and most probably very recent.

Jere and Leo took Tom back to Lamar. The rest of us drove south of McClave, to the place where Paul thinks the Carter Sand and Gravel Company might be endangering the trail. We showed the site to John Paige and Don Hill. Then we moved on to Hasty and south to the John Martin Reservoir. The Corps of Engineers has fenced off an area there where there are faint ruts, so faint that I couldn't see them at all. I was going to ignore them for the map book until Jere said that he had visited the place after a snowstorm last November, and the ruts were visible when covered with snow. The soil is so powdery and so given to blowing that I don't see how they could have lasted this long.

We drove toward the dam and cut off toward the picnic area. Looking high to the left we saw the curious, spindly, flat-topped rock formations, known as Red Shin's Standing Ground. Paul says he has documentation for this story: Red Shins, a Cheyenne brave, fell in disfavor with some other braves over a woman. They set out to kill him. He retreated from the nearby Arkansas River to the rock formation now named for him and successfully defended his position.

We continued on to the new Fort Lyon, now the site of a big Veteran's Administration medical center, some six miles east of Las Animas. There Paul took us in tow, as Betty and I really wanted to see the Kit Carson Chapel. It wasn't always a chapel. In fact, it was the post surgeon's office in 1868 when Carson was brought in with a lung disorder. He had returned on the railroad from Washington, D.C., as far as Cheyenne, then he had taken a stage as far as Boggsville. He was terribly ill, so the surgeon urged him to come to the fort while the river was still fordable. Carson died in his office.

In 1957, before many Americans had heard the word

"preservation," the building was converted to a chapel. A stone vestibule was added to the front; the second story was removed and a steep gable roof added, along with a steeple. In the process, the historic building was totally ruined. Only the walls are original.

We visited a couple of other stone buildings on the fort— these being essentially unaltered from the 1860s—then headed for the motel. After Paul checked in we continued south through Las Animas to the cemetery a mile or so south of town. As we drove in the gates, a dozen or so turkey buzzards circled high above our cars. There, in the southeast corner, was the grave of William Bent, the great pioneer who died here in 1869. We had seen the grave of his brother, Charles Bent, in Santa Fe a couple of weeks ago. Now here was William. Two of the great names of the Santa Fe Trail.

We continued on to the southeast and came to the "town" of Boggsville. Here Thomas O. Boggs built a great U-shaped house of adobe. Behind it is the two-story home of John W. Prowers, a local pioneer. Both buildings are in decrepit shape. The site was recently acquired by the Bent County Historical Society, but they need an angel to get those buildings stabilized, let alone restored to museum status.

Tuesday, May 17, 1988

During breakfast we were richly entertained by Paul Bentrup, who brought along a copy of Mary Jean Cook's book about the Loretto Sisters in Santa Fe. Theirs is the chapel where a "mysterious carpenter" built their freestanding

Paul Bentrup

The marker at Bent's New Fort. An old iron bridge over the Arkansas appears faintly at left.

spiral stair, then disappeared before he could be thanked. Legend says it was St. Joseph himself, but Cook has tracked down the probable carpenter.

Paul gave me a couple of photographs. One was of the newly mounted sign erected by the Kansas State Historical Society at "Paul's Ruts," the ground he had donated to the local historical society. The other shot was of his ruts after a light snowfall. They were highlighted beautifully.

Jere and John Paige joined us. John has had to learn a great deal in a very short period of time. This morning he was fully relaxed and seemed to be enjoying our company. If you can't relax around Paul Bentrup you can't relax at all. Leo and Bonita arrived and we were once again ready to hit the trail.

Paul Bentrup

The Kansas State Historical Society erected this sign at "Paul's Ruts" in 1988.

Snow highlights the ruts on the land Paul Bentrup donated to the Kearny County Museum.

We were off to Bent's Old Fort, where Jere said we'd have two hours to gawk. Could it have been only twenty-seven hours ago that I had done this very thing? How different it was today. The farmsteads were awake. Instead of only an orange glow in the rear view mirror, the sun was high and the land was warm and throbbing with life.

I looked at the trees lining the Arkansas River. In most cases the riverbanks were devoid of trees in trail days. Not so here. This spot is at the west end of a forty-five-mile long band of woods known as "Big Timbers."

We were on the road only seven or eight minutes when I was shocked by a giant "swoosh." I looked to the left and saw a B-52 bomber, flying at no more than 1,000 feet.

I wondered what kind of maneuvers were going on. The plane flew several miles south, then banked gently to the right.

At the fort Don Hill explained that a bombing range is nearby and is frequented by B-52s and B-1s. One of the latter went down near La Junta not long ago.

This was my third visit to the fort and the first time I was able to go inside. I have often said that Fort Laramie, on the Oregon Trail in Wyoming, is the crown jewel of the National Park Service. Indeed it is, but there must be room in that crown for two jewels. Add Bent's Old Fort.

The inner courtyard was smaller than I had envisioned it, probably because all photographers use wide-angle lenses to shoot it. I climbed up to the rooftop level and shot in four directions, in color and black-and-white. Then to ground level to do the same, mostly through doorways as framing devices. Not only is the reconstruction accurate, the rooms are furnished as they would have been in Bent's day.

The beauty is skin deep, however. Don complained about the leaky roofs. His maintenance people are having to strip them down to the bare concrete and resurface them with materials which will not accept and hold water. It is a huge job.

In a caravan of four vehicles, we followed Highway 350 to the west. It was a lovely stretch of road. On the left, the grasslands were greening. They stretched as far as I could see. On the right there was the Santa Fe Railroad. The West is so grand, with broad vistas that give me such feelings of elation, of freedom, of creativity—I wonder why I live in the Midwest. And in a city, to boot.

A fur press is at right in the courtyard of Bent's Old Fort.

Courtyard and main gate of Bent's Old Fort

The land was beginning to break up as we headed to the southwest. On the horizon ahead and to the left were the three cones described by Marc Simmons. The stage road to Santa Fe passed through a gap just to the right of them.

About ten miles southwest of Timpas I saw Jere's tail lights glowing. He turned left onto a gravel road. We followed, drove south only a mile and stopped. A dozen head of curious cattle eyed us from a few yards away. Paul got out of his truck waving his blue coat as a matador's cape and singing the "Toreador Song."

We were at the Iron Springs. On the left were two stock tanks; to the south was a square concrete enclosure. Beneath that flowed the spring, which was piped to one of the tanks. In a hurry as always to get a good picture, I wasn't watching where I was going, and what I slid into wasn't second base. Let's hope it will wear off. (It did.)

I parted the decaying planks atop the concrete enclosure; the water four feet below looked pretty slimy and appeared to be stagnant. To the south was what obviously had been the foundations of a small rock building. I thought that that might have been the site of the Iron Springs Stage Station, but was told that scattered rocks just west of the stock tanks marked that site. Stage stations usually had more than one structure. This was an auxiliary building of some sort.

Another sixteen miles brought us to what was once the settlement of Thatcher. What a disaster! One house was almost totally devoid of a roof. Across the dusty gravel road was a stuccoed house, roof more or less intact, but with all its windows broken out. Next to it was all that remains of the Thatcher School. This was no one-room country

John Paige at the site of one of the buildings of the Iron Springs Stage Station.

schoolhouse, but a building which would have been at home in any city. Most of the windows were now gone and the area was littered with trash. The building was apparently being used for storage by the rancher who lived to the rear.

In front of the school a VW sedan sat with most of its tires flat. Nearby were a '60s-vintage Cadillac with all four tires down and a yellow Pinto. Its tires, too, were flat. A broken-down truck was parked in a bay of the school, obviously not operable.

What happened to Thatcher? Where were its people?

We parked at the tail end of what was once a broad reservoir, backed up by a dam constructed by the Santa Fe Railroad. We walked to the west, toward the dam site, on a carpet of silt several feet thick which had built up in the days before the project had been abandoned (like everything else around here) and the reservoir went dry. Beneath that silt is the rock floor of trail days, and somewhere in that rock floor is the famous Hole in the Rock and the foundations of the Hole in the Rock Stage Station.

The Hole in the Rock was a nearly circular opening filled with spring water of fathomless depth. We will never know now where it was. The dam is one impressive structure, stretching between the deep walls of the Timpas Creek canyon.

Another seventeen miles toward Trinidad and we passed the settlement of Model. I thought it should be pronounced mo-DEL, but I found out it is pronounced MO-del. Near here is another mystery—Hole in the Prairie. This was evidently a small lake by the Hole in the Prairie Stage Station. We couldn't find it.

Along the way to Trinidad we stopped a couple of times to photograph Fisher's Peak.

From the motel we followed Jere's Taurus, now carrying not only John Paige but Mark Gardner, administrator of the Baca-Bloom houses and our escort for the next couple of days.

I first met Mark in Hutchinson. He is on the Santa Fe Trail Association board of directors. Very young, very sharp, and very modest. Katie Davis was with him then. Now Mark told us they have set their wedding date for September and will honeymoon on the Cumbres and Toltec Railroad. That is a steam train that I have longed to ride for many years.

At the conclusion of the Hutchinson symposium, Mark put on his fur hat, grabbed his banjo, and entertained the crowd with period songs for an hour. A couple of months later, after he learned we were going to publish the Brown manuscript on the SFT, he contacted me to see if I would correct an error that was in the original report. A quote pertaining to the Last Chance Store actually referred to the Conn Store.

Mark is a guy who even looks historical. He wears his hair long, sports a goatee and mustache, and wears those wire-rimmed glasses that were worn a hundred years ago. He gets very excited about his research—on SFT merchants—and talks so fast it requires concentration to follow him.

He took us to a spring a couple of miles from town, with a little oral history behind it. The owner says that his father told him that his grandfather, who was a captain on a wagon train, stopped at this spring. Maybe so. Nobody is certain how the trail proceeded through Trinidad, but it had to come through somewhere, and this might be as good a place as any.

I had heard about an equestrian statue of Kit Carson in a Trinidad park named for Carson. Mark led the way. It is magnificent; a wonderful heroic bronze that dominates the hill.

Neither Leo nor Jere had ever been to the Stonewall. This time I led the way west of town on Highway 12 to that unique geological formation and the location of the Marion Russell ranch for so many years. It started to sprinkle as soon as we got there. We drove up to the little Russell cemetery to visit again the graves of the Russell family.

Dinner this night was at Trinidad's La Fiesta. We were

This statue of Kit Carson is in Trinidad's Kit Carson Park.

joined there by Richard Louden, who would be our guide on the military road, and his brother Willard. Richard is soft-spoken and extremely articulate. He wants to preserve the military road through Emery Gap.

The Stonewall

The graves of Marion Russell, center, and her husband, Richard, right.

Wednesday, May 18, 1988

We were supposed to be at the old Wootton place at 8 A.M. and just made it. The owners of the ranch there, Mr. and Mrs. Don Berg, said we could stay until ten, when they had to leave.

I had wondered about Don Berg. The word I had was that after Uncle Dick Wootton's adobe house burned, he felt there was no way to preserve it and had bulldozed what was left.

We drove to the pass and Berg met us at the gate. He is in his seventies; his walk is assisted by a cane. The others swarmed about him when we got there; I remained in the car while he opened the gate. As our car was going through the gate he smiled and gave us a friendly wave. As soon as our car got through I left the wheel and went back to introduce myself. He was warm and friendly, and seemed genuinely glad to see us. My feelings of hostility for having bulldozed the house vanished immediately.

I followed Jere's car with John and Mark up the pass. Leo and Bonita were riding with us. The radios crackled between the cars. Beside the road we found the lonely grave of Cruz Torrez, the U.S. Cavalry soldier who was murdered in 1868, three years after Richens Lacy (''Uncle Dick'') Wootton opened his toll road through the pass. Leo said he had read an account to the effect that Uncle Dick had heard the firing from his ranch, but that would have been remarkable, as the house is two miles away. We stopped to photograph the grave, then continued on up the pass. After we had passed through two more gates we finally arrived at the high point, where the tracks of the Santa Fe enter a tunnel bored beneath Raton Pass.

The land has been so worked up there, by the railroad and by subsequent road builders, that there is no way to know today where the trail is. My companions hiked up in search of it anyway, as I had done last March.

I walked down to the portal of the tunnel. A concrete obelisk announced "New Mexico" on one side and "Colorado" on the other. There was obviously ventilation in the tunnel, but the smell of diesel oil was strong. The walls were stained with soot from the burned fuel, as was the tunnel entrance.

I wanted a train to come along—so did the explorers now atop the tunnel—but none was to be heard. It was perfectly quiet. We drove back to the ranch buildings of the Bergs.

Don met us outside. All of us asked several questions about the place. I learned that the handsome adobe barn was not Uncle Dick's at all. It had been built in 1908 by the J. P. Morgan interests when they had owned the ranch. I asked about the house itself, trying to verify that it had been bulldozed away.

"Oh, a good bit of it is still here. Want to see it?" he asked. Surprised, I nodded in agreement. He led us behind his handsome new double-wide mobile home. There was a large structure in back with modern sheathing. We went inside and into his well-appointed office, with a rolltop desk as large as my own. There were several pictures on the wall of the ranch as it used to be.

He explained how it became necessary to take down the remains of what was Uncle Dick's house, but he was able to save the single-story portion, which had not burned. That is where we stood.

Adobe barn of J. P. Morgan

Headstone of Cruz Torrez

Rut swale in Raton Pass

Don told us a story about Uncle Dick that he learned as a youngster when his parents were running the ranch. An old gentleman who had known Uncle Dick a half century earlier told him that a traveler passing through on the toll road noticed that the roof of the Wootton ranchhouse building was afire. He rushed to the house and pounded on the door to alert Uncle Dick and together they managed to get the fire out. The traveler was about to leave when Uncle Dick said, "Wait a minute." He then charged the toll.

Don Berg answered our questions for a good half hour. Although his family had been in the Raton area since the 1920s, he was the first to own the property. He loved that land and cared for it, and it showed.

I asked about the wagon road over the pass. "Which

Remains of the Wootton house

one?'' he responded. ''All the roads up here changed every few years. When they were surveying for I-25 back in the sixties, I told the chief engineer that the roads never lasted more than twenty years up here, as better ways to cross were discovered. So I asked him, 'Why don't you just eliminate this step and put the road along Chicken Creek?' He laughed and said, 'You know, Don, that probably is a pretty good idea, as that does seem to be the better way to go.'''

We drove back downtown and picked up Willard Louden, then we headed out toward the military road, northeast of town. Now the radios came to life. Willard dazzled us with his knowledge of the area—history, archaeology, geology, paleontology, botany, ornithology. He fascinated us with the story of the discovery of dinosaur tracks in the Jurassic rocks near here. His commentary entertained us for the length of the trip.

He told us of the line of mesas which stretched from west of Trinidad all the way to the Oklahoma Panhandle, and how they were pierced by the several passes which accommodated the settlement of the Southwest: the Raton, here at Trinidad; the Trinchera, which took the Goodnight-Loving cattle trail through; Emery Gap, which took the military road through; and the Marco Burro, or Lame Burro.

We passed along one cut, heading east, and framed in the center of it was Sierra Grande. It was the better part of a month ago that I stood on the Santa Fe tracks opposite Round Mound and shot Sierra Grande, while we were traveling the Cimarron Cutoff with Bill Wheatley. Then we were seeing it from the east. Now we saw it from the north. Willard mentioned Nigger Mesa and said that cartographers had recently changed its name to Black Mesa. He gave this comment without laughter or explanation.

About twenty miles to the east we turned right on a gravel road where a small sign announced: ''Louden Cattle Co. 18 mi.'' There was a new Ford pickup on the shoulder of the road a few miles to the south; Richard Louden was waiting for us.

The two brothers obviously own a lot of land here. Richard does the active ranching; Willard lives in Trinidad. Richard pointed to the northwest. We could see a snake-like path of green, leading to the gap in the hills. ''That's the old military road,'' he said, ''leading right for Emery Gap over there.''

The team seeking the military road, from left: Mark Gardner, Richard Louden, Willard Louden, Leo Oliva, John Paige, and Jere Krakow.

Richard has a degree in journalism ("I decided I'd rather be a cowboy," he said), while Willard has degrees in geology, psychology, and art. His landscapes have been displayed at several prestigious Western art shows.

We drove to a field where we parked our cars and got into the bed of Richard's new pickup. Then we lurched over perhaps three miles of the military road, heading for Purgatoire Canyon. The road was very faint; a blowout or water-eroded ditch here and there, but for the most part, only a faint trace across the prairie.

We parked at the edge of the canyon. Betty and I stayed near the truck; the rest hiked a quarter-mile on to the northeast. They were gone more than an hour, looking at the ruts up there but mostly just talking. I was irritated. This was no longer research, but pure recreation. We are here to do a job, not to stand around on one leg and talk.

Furthermore, I was stewing about the idea of cluttering up the map book with obscure trails. This particular one especially. It is defined in part by Glenn Scott in his fine USGS maps, which are on sale today. No more than a handful of people would ever be interested in it. The same goes for the Aubry Route, but there is a little more justification for including that one, since it is not mapped anywhere that is available to the general public. Yes, this is an impressive experience. No, it doesn't belong in a popular book of the Santa Fe Trail, and I plan to protest its inclusion.

I have a compromise in mind. If the National Park Service wants this included, we could provide Xerox copies of the pages to be given out with their report, but I am not inclined to put it in the map book which we are publishing. Our duty is to show the Santa Fe Trail. That we are committed to do. No more.

We drove down through Emery Gap, down to a little stone building which had been the toll house when this was a toll road. Richard told of a fellow from Springfield, Colorado, who was poking around here recently with a metal detector and uncovered a dutch oven filled with silver coins.

We took the Folsom road past the site of the then-startling discovery of evidence of Folsom Man, human beings who had occupied this land ten thousand years ago. And on we went into the town of Raton.

The Chrysler had developed a new problem—the orange light went on, telling me we were about out of gas. We circled around in one little burg, but there was no gas station there. We had no choice but to try to get to Raton. It started to rain as we climbed Johnson Mesa, and then to pour. The roads were narrow and winding. It was not the time or the place to run out of gas. Suddenly I became very fond of those ornery radios.

We came upon three mounted cowboys driving a herd of several hundred cattle down the center of the road. Panting dogs, with smiles on their faces a yard wide, were helping. Gradually the cowboys moved the herd to one side to allow our cars to pass through, waving as we went by. Friendly country.

We rolled to a station in Raton with the needle to the left of the empty mark. The car took just seventeen gallons, so there was still more than a gallon in the tank. Nonetheless, it was a good feeling to see that needle on the peg on the other side of the gauge.

The town of Raton isn't ratty at all. It is a clean, well-kept place. We drove to the Amtrak depot. Most of us wanted to ride the train over Raton Pass to Trinidad. Leo ordered the tickets and we learned that the 6:07 would be an hour late. That was fine with us. It gave us time to look at the WPA murals in the Chamber of Commerce Building, then go to Clifton House, and maybe even to Willow Spring.

After looking at the extremely well-done murals, which depict scenes from the early history of Raton, we drove south on I-25 to the U.S. 64 exit, looked some three-quarters of a mile to the right, and saw a large and erect hunk of adobe—all that remains of Clifton House.

We hiked over the field, up and over the old railroad embankment, and then down to the little Canadian. Unfortunately, the river was a tad too large to cross without getting my feet wet. Then we hiked the last quarter-mile or so to the ruin.

Clifton House had been a huge hostelry on the trail, surrounded by a level campground with lots of wood and live water. Now it was a single column of adobe on a stone foundation, a monolith ten feet high and about four feet wide. How long would it last? Maybe it will take another ten years of weathering before a strong wind, or the hand of the omnipresent vandal, will take it down.

I couldn't find the normal linear mounds of melted adobe, such as are at old Fort Hall on the Oregon Trail. That was curious, as it had been a huge, three-story building. But the first story might have been stone, a full story, rather than what appeared to be a foundation today. That would mean that the melt now is several feet deep and level across the onetime cavity formed by the stone foundation.

We drove back to Raton and to Willow Spring, the site of a onetime stage station. There, at 545 Railroad Avenue, was a neat little house with a well-manicured lawn. Iron gates at the driveway had the words ''Willow Spring'' formed in welded steel. A wooden ''Willow Spring'' sign swung at the entrance.

Mr. and Mrs. Willie Gaskin answered our knock at their back door. We asked if we could see the Willow Spring. ''Well, you're looking at it,'' answered Gaskin.

There, in a corner of the concrete walkway, were several aluminum-painted pipes atop a steel plate. That plate covered Willow Spring.

''Turn on the pump, Willie,'' said his wife. ''Show 'em

At Willow Spring, from left: Betty Burnett, John Paige, Willie Gaskin, Leo Oliva, Jere Krakow, Bonita Oliva, and Mrs. Gaskin.

how it works.'' Willie opened a panel box and threw a switch. We heard an electric motor running. He turned a spigot at the end of one of the pipes and a rush of water came out.

In the meantime, Mrs. Gaskin had gone into the house to get several plastic cups. ''Here, try it. See if you like it.'' We all had a drink from Willow Spring. The water was clear, cool, tasteless. The Gaskins smiled to see our pleasure. She went back in the house to emerge with a stereoptican viewer and a slide of Willow Spring at the time the railroad came through. The scene, which was a promotion of the Santa Fe Railroad, showed a long, low ranch-house with the sign Willow Spring on it. There was no indication of the photographer. I wondered if it could have been William Henry Jackson.

We still had a little time before our train ride. We headed up Moulton Street and climbed high above the town on a remarkably good gravel road. We went some ten miles, nearly into the pass, when the way was blocked by a fence of barbed wire and enormous boulders, a case of overkill if I ever saw one. We turned around and drove back to Raton, enjoying some thrilling views—thrilling because there were no guard rails between the road and the frightening chasms below.

We arrived at the station with about fifteen minutes to spare. Promptly at 7:25 the headlight popped into view. A friendly conductor welcomed us aboard. The trip lasted an hour and gave us a new perspective on the pass. It doesn't take many flights on commercial airliners to realize that Amtrak is a fine way to go.

Thursday, May 19, 1988

It rained most of the night. It was a cold, hard drizzle and there wasn't much heat in the room. I could feel the chill.

Mary Lee DeGarbo, a local historian, had called Mark Gardner when she heard we were in town and offered to direct us to some ruts near her home in Hoehne, north of Trinidad. We drove out to pick her up about eight o'clock. She first showed us some deep swales alongside a fence, but I was sure this was a farm road. As Leo said, the tracks were too close together and going in the wrong direction. But soon we saw the McCoy: a single broad, deep swale, very similar to the one in Minor Park in Kansas City. It was filled with trash—old tires, an abandoned stove, an old refrigerator. Nearly a quarter-mile of junk in the best ruts we had seen in a long time.

We were able to follow them for about eight miles to the northeast, almost as far as Model, and wherever we could see the route of the Santa Fe Trail, ruts were visible.

Mary Lee took us next to the outskirts of El Moro, far to the south. There we talked with a woman who has a DAR marker in her farmyard. This site had been the busy El Moro depot in 1910, when the DAR dedicated the marker. Now the railroad tracks are gone and so is the depot. Nothing was left but the marker. Someone dug up its huge rock foundation and moved it and the stone a few yards away from the original position. Now the woman wants it moved back. She showed us two photographs taken during the dedication, long before her house was built. She's proud of those pictures, proud of that marker, and proud to be able to say she lives on the Santa Fe Trail.

As we headed west, the rain was unceasing. The mountains (really the foothills of the Sangre de Cristo) were drenched with dripping clouds, their peaks invisible. Our next destination was Cimarron.

We passed the Whittington Center of the National Rifle Association—the extensive grounds have many miles of the Santa Fe Trail and a lot of visible ruts.

Lucien Maxwell moved to Cimarron in 1857 and made it headquarters for his land grant of two million acres. We went in to the old but recently restored St. James Hotel.

Lucien Maxwell's house in Rayado is guarded by a goofy little dog.

It is just gorgeous. It began in 1873 as a saloon. Seven years later it became a hotel. Their literature says that twenty-six men were killed within those adobe walls. Ed and Pat Sitzberger restored it and reopened it in 1985.

At lunch we met the Sitzbergers and their guest, Robert L. Thomas, the outdoor editor of the *Arizona Republic* in Phoenix.

We walked around Cimarron, taking pictures as we went, and we toured the museum in the old stone mill. Then we took off for Rayado.

We first visited the famous Philmont Scout Ranch, where Jere paid a social call on the director of the museum. South of town we saw some badly eroded swales. We surmounted the hill and parked at a little turnout there.

At Rayado out trotted that goofy little dog who had barked her fool head off the last time we were here to take a picture of Lucien Maxwell's house. This time she was skittish; I finally got her to trust me enough to let me rub her stomach.

We walked down the street to see the old Kit Carson home, now rebuilt and completely stripped of its historical worth. The Philmont officials knew no better at that time. Now they do. In fact, they are abandoning Rayado as an active Scout activity center and plan to use the place as a historical tract from now on. Maybe they can re-restore the Carson house.

A couple of mule deer circled the building and emerged on the north side to break into a trot and cross the road. They came to the barbed wire fence. Each leapt high, seemingly levitating over the fence, and loped out across the field. A herd of a dozen riding horses investigated, then turned tail and they were out of sight.

Continuing south from Rayado we looked to the left and saw a gap over a lake. That should be the route of the trail coming from the Rock Crossing of the Canadian, to Taos. I thought of Sue and Joe Knowles at the Dos Rios Ranch, where the trails split. One branch went to Santa Fe; the other to Taos.

I looked over my right shoulder and saw a big, deep canyon. That is what sheltered the route of the caravans as they threaded their way over the ridge to the old Spanish mission settlement.

Before we took off through the rain for Taos I called the highway patrol, just to be on the safe side.

"No problem," the officer said. "It never snows up there this time of year."

We went, climbing high into what appeared to be the clouds. But when we got up there, they still weren't touching the ground.

Taos was obviously an attractive town at one time, now gone bad. We tourists did it. Once it was a sleepy, otherworldly place. Now it bustles as great sums change hands. Art galleries have proliferated and the souvenir business is booming. See this. See that. Pay. Pay. Pay.

Even the Indians have the problem. To see Taos Pueblo, one must pay a personal admission charge, a parking fee, and a surcharge for cameras. Otherwise it's no admittance. They can extort all they want to, but they will never extort me. You can shove it, Lo.

We photographed the great mission church of San Francisco de Asis. What a gorgeous thing that is. I lay flat in the plaza and shot through the arched gate. At the state park I shot Kit Carson's grave. Next to him is his wife, Josefa. Then I photographed the homes of Governor Charles Bent and Kit Carson.

During dinner I agreed to include that darned military road we had explored yesterday, as well as the Aubry Cutoff. I also agreed to show the Taos route from the Rock Crossing of the Canadian in one small-scale map. How can you say no to guys like Jere and Leo? Furthermore, I felt good about it.

We came back across the pass in more rain. Tomorrow will be the last day of this odyssey.

Friday, May 20, 1988

Again it was cool and still lightly sprinkling rain as I packed the car getting ready to go to the Ocate Crossing. A tall, slender guy came out of the restaurant and Jere in-

Church of San Francisco de Asis, Taos

troduced me to Ron Johnson, an outdoor recreation planner and John Paige's boss in Denver. He was accompanied
by his friend, Mary Fransa. Betty had compiled the
historical component of a report on the area in East St.
Louis opposite the Jefferson National Expansion Memorial
for Ron, so they were acquainted.

Jere called the foreman of the Fort Union Ranch at 5:30
this morning. He advised us that we could never get a car
on those ranch roads to see the ruts, after the soaker they
had and were still getting. Furthermore, he would rather
we didn't take a 4x4 out there either, as it would tend to
tear up the roads. Jere agreed.

We went slowly through the hills to Rayado, then on
to Springer. I noticed that the mesas were capped with a
light dusting of snow; snow that hadn't been there yesterday. Ron Johnson's car was in the lead, followed by the
Taurus, then the Chrysler, then Bonita in the camper and
Leo in the motor home. I called Jere and Ron on the radio:
"Five vehicles now; we're beginning to look more and more
like a funeral."

Jere replied, "Turn on your lights, Gregory."

I remarked to Betty, "I sure hope Jere doesn't get any
ideas about going to the Santa Clara Spring this morning."

The radio crackled. "Do you copy, Gregory?"

"You bet."

"What do you say we have another go at Santa Clara
Spring this morning?"

I said that we really ought to get to Ocate before the
weather got any worse. Besides, I had a lot to do in Santa
Fe before the day was over. We proceeded to Ocate.

After we had gone thirteen miles I looked to the right

and saw the neat ranch buildings nestled up against the mesa wall to the north. But Jere kept going into the little settlement of Ocate. I presumed that he knew where he was going. That was not a very good assumption. We pulled into the parking lot of the Ocate post office to discuss our whereabouts. I told him I thought we'd passed the crossing. We verified it with the copy of Brown that Leo had in his camper.

This time I took the lead. There was the familiar mailbox, "Mora Ranch." I turned in on the red clay road. Oh-oh. I backed up. I suggested that Leo and I take his 4x4 camper down to the place where I thought the crossing was. I remembered that the road crosses the route of the trail and an eroded rut swale just a few yards before a wood bridge goes over Ocate Creek. (That is pronounced O'-ca-*tay,* by the way.)

We slithered down the road for about two miles. We crossed the creek just as I remembered it, but I didn't see the ruts. We turned left and drove another mile to the buildings. There I met Harold J. Slater, who had worked on the ranch for most of his adult life. He verified that the trail came around the point of the mesa and crossed just where I said it did. I couldn't understand why I couldn't see it.

We returned to the crossing. There were the ruts, right where I had remembered they were. They are hard to see from the south, easy to see when heading north. Everything checked out now. We drove back to the highway and it was time to split up.

We shook hands good-bye all around and Betty and I headed for Santa Fe as the camper slid down the road toward the crossing.

In Santa Fe we stopped at Mission San Miguel—now there's a church! A member of the order of Christian Brothers sat just inside the door, a gentle, smiling, loving man who answered our questions politely and encouraged me to take all the photographs I wanted.

The building is alleged to be the oldest church in the United States, with construction having started in 1610. The walls are original. In an adjacent room, now a gift shop, another Christian Brother repeated for me the story of the old church bell, believed cast in 1356, when the Moors were being chased out of Spain. He played it for me, as he surely has for countless thousands of others. But he did so as if I were the first one he had told this story to.

Then we went to the Chapel of Our Lady of Light, formerly staffed by the Loretto order but now a tourist spot. We had read about it earlier in *Loretto* by Mary Jean Straw (Cook).

Off, in a driving rain, to the Palace of the Governors, where we called on Orlando Romero, the fine scholar who had offered me assistance in the Santa Fe Trail study some months ago. I wanted to ask Orlando his opinion of the photograph of the grave of Sr. Mary Alphonso Thompson on the Santa Fe Trail. He couldn't answer our questions, but directed us to the photo archives, where I happened to see Evelyn Vinogradov, Marc Simmons's friend from Denver. She was so glad to see me she came over and gave me a big hug.

After a lot more questions, but very few answers, we went back out in the rain, across the Plaza, and admired the work in a couple of the fine art shops.

The altar of Mission San Miguel

Then we sloshed back to the car and headed back to I-25. In Raton Pass there was snow on the mountain tops, and a heavy rain battered the windshield. But not for long. Soon it became snow. The warmth and comfort of the car certainly felt good. I was riding in shirtsleeves at sixty miles an hour over a mountain pass in the snow. How different this was from the days of the wagons.

Hardly a thought was given to the fact that the expedition was now history. The sadness, I knew, would come later.

Saturday, May 21, 1988

We decided to stay on I-25 all the way to Colorado Springs, then head up toward Limon and get on I-70 there, to roar comfortably across the eastern plains of Colorado, Kansas, and Missouri in two days.

The morning began with bright sunshine. I looked up at Fisher's Peak—that's what I wanted! A couple of inches of snow on that old flat top perched against a blue sky.

As we headed north on I-25, the great peaks of the Front Range gave us a thrilling view. The symmetry of Mount Blanca was inspiring, even though the peak itself was enshrouded with clouds.

We drove up to Limon, Colorado, to hit I-25. Along the way we encountered extremely high winds from the north. The sky around us was indigo. The rain splattered against the windshield. Whirlpools of it centered on my side window; the rushing air spinning it vertically, in defiance of gravity. Tumbleweeds shot across the rust-colored pavement, heading for fields which looked as if they were boiling. The driving rain splattered in the mud.

We drove out of the rain momentarily, and then into a series of storms. The wipers seldom were off, all the way to Hays, Kansas, where we stopped for our last night on the road.

Sunday, May 22, 1988

I suppose the ranchers needed it, this rain, but I certainly have had enough. It came down in drizzles, it came down in torrents, but never, not until we approached St. Louis, did it not come down at all.

We pulled up in front of the office at 7:14 P.M. It was over.

EPILOG

As we drove east my thoughts had centered on the experience of the past nine weeks. The morning we all met for the first day of the effort, at the Santa Fe Restaurant in Boonville. Yes, there was a sadness associated with the ending of the effort. But there was joy, too, thinking of the wonderful people I had met in those weeks. Their intelligence and knowledge kept me in a constant state of surprise. Some were formally trained in distinguished graduate schools. Some didn't even get out of grade school.

They were gentle people, these Santa Fe Trail buffs and scholars and landowners; kind people, people who cared about us and about those who rolled over the trail in covered wagons. Did anybody say no to us? Only one, a man in great personal distress at the time. Without that expedition I would not have been acquainted with any of them.

But it is Jere, Bonita, and Leo whom I shall miss. Sweet Bonita who could wear the legs off a mountain goat. We would get out of the car to look at some swales, look up, and Bonita would be a quarter-mile away, trying to trace the ruts to the end.

And Leo—what a workhorse! His Ph.D. shows. He simply amazed me with his knowledge of the trail and the people who took it. He has a joyful sense of humor. Last week, for example, in his attempt to get his soy beans planted, he worked through lunch and often didn't get to the house for dinner until after ten at night. "What did you have for lunch?" I asked him. "Soy beans," he answered.

He has a spirit of willingness that defies conflict; he wants no part of that. Leo is obviously a deeply satisfied man.

And Jere. It was hard to catch that guy when he wasn't smiling. He told me this was the most exciting assignment he had ever had with the National Park Service. I'll bet it was. Jere likes to take his time with people. By not rushing through this project, as I would have done, he has brought in a research program of superb quality. The idea of being escorted to the swales and historic sites by the landowners is a good one. He didn't do the study quickly; he did it carefully. Jere is a fine man and I would like to work with him again.

Now it is over. We will meet once again for a critique of my own map work; that should be interesting, even fun. But it will not be the same. The weeks of discovery, exciting discovery, are now over. I wish it could have lasted forever.

INDEX

Two wonderful associations
to enchance enjoyment of the trails:

The Santa Fe Trail Association

Your membership will
- [ ] Help with efforts to preserve the remaining ruts of the Santa Fe Trail and associated historic sites.
- [ ] Bring you four thrilling issues of *Wagon Tracks* each year, news of the association and the trail
- [ ] Enable you to attend the conventions and conferences of the association, and
  - [ ] enjoy field trips out on the trail
  - [ ] hear thrilling papers about the trail
  - [ ] enjoy the camaradarie of fellow trail students and scholars

OREGON-CALIFORNIA TRAILS ASSOCIATION

Your membership will
- [ ] Help save the remaining traces of the trail and related historic sites
- [ ] Bring you four issues of the *Overland Journal* and four issues of *News From the Plains* each year
- [ ] Enable you to attend OCTA conventions in historic trail cities each year, featuring
  - [ ] Field trips to important trail sites
  - [ ] Wonderful slide shows and papers on the trail and its history
  - [ ] Companionship of new and interesting trail friends

For a free membership application
to both trails associations,
call toll-free: 1-800-367-9242

Other Western Books Published or Marketed by The Patrice Press

These books may be purchased by direct mail. Order from:

The Patrice Press
1701 South Eighth St., St. Louis, MO 63104

There is a $2.95 shipping and handling charge for the first book and a 95-cent charge for each additional book. Missourians please add 6.1% sales tax.

You may call toll-free to place your order:
1-800-367-9242.

AMERICAN HISTORY

Exploring the American West, 1803-1879, William Goetzmann. 128 pages. Paper, $7.95

Indian, Soldier, and Settler, Robert M. Utley. 84 pages. Paper, $7.95

Kansas in Maps, Robert W. Baughman. 104 pages. Cloth, $14.95

The Beginning of the West, Louise Barry. 1296 pages. Cloth, $14.75

The Latter-day Saints' Emigrants' Guide, Wm. Clayton; Stanley B. Kimball, Ph.D., ed. 107 pages. Paper, $19.95, ISBN: 0-935284-27-3.

The Overland Migrations, David Lavender. 111 pages. Paper, $7.95

THE OREGON-CALIFORNIA TRAIL

Emigrant Trails West, Helfrich/Hunt. 211 pages. Paper, $19.95

Fort Laramie, David Lavender. 159 pages. Paper, $8.95

Fort Vancouver, David Lavender. 143 pages. Paper, $8.95

Forty-niners, Archer Butler Hulbert. 340 pages. Paper, $14.95

Ghost Trails to California, Tom Hunt. 288 pages, 8½″ x 11″. Cloth, $34.95; paper, $22.95

Historic Sites Along the Oregon Trail, Aubrey L. Haines. 439 pages. Cloth, $24.95, ISBN: 0-935284-50-8. Paper, $12.95, ISBN: 0-935284-51-6.

Historic Sites and Markers Along the Mormon and Other Great Western Trails, Stanley B. Kimball. 320 pages. Cloth, $37.95; paper, $15.95.

Maps of the Oregon Trail, Gregory M. Franzwa. 292 pages. Cloth, $24.95, ISBN: 0-935284-30-3. Paper, $14.95, ISBN: 0-935284-32-X. Looseleaf, $27.95, ISBN: 0-935284-31-1.

Oregon Trail map 16" x 24", $2.95

Overland to California with the Pioneer Line; The Gold Rush Diary of Bernard K. Reid, ed. by Mary McDougall Gordon. 246 pages. Paper, $14.95

Platte River Road Narratives, Merrill J. Mattes. 672 pages, 8½" x 11". Cloth, $95

Pump on the Prairie, Musetta Gilman. 223 pages. Paper, $12.95

Scotts Bluff, Merrill J. Mattes. 64 pages. Paper, $2.45

The Great Platte River Road, Merrill J. Mattes. 583 pages. Cloth, $36.95; paper, $16.95

The Oregon Trail Revisited, Gregory M. Franzwa. 419 pages. Cloth, $14.95, ISBN: 0-935284-57-5. Paper, $7.95, ISBN: 0-935284-58-3.

The Wake of the Prairie Schooner, Irene D. Paden. 514 pages. Cloth, $24.95, ISBN: 0-935284-40-0. Paper, $12.95, ISBN:0-935284-38-9.

Trail of the First Wagons Over the Sierra Nevada, Charles K. Graydon. 81 pages. Paper, $12.95, ISBN: 0-935284-47-8

To the Land of Gold and Wickedness: The 1848-59 Diary of Lorena Hays, Jeanne Watson, ed. 496 pages. Cloth, $27.95, ISBN: 0-935284-53-2.

Whitman Mission, Erwin N. Thompson. 92 pages. Paper, $4.45

THE SANTA FE TRAIL

Following the Santa Fe Trail, Marc Simmons, Ph.D. 214 pages. Paper, $12.95

Images of the Santa Fe Trail, Gregory M. Franzwa. 114 photographs. Cloth, $24.95, ISBN: 0-935284-60-5. Paper, $19.95, ISBN: 0-935284-61-3.

Impressions of The Santa Fe Trail: A Contemporary Diary, Gregory M. Franzwa. 207 pages. Cloth, $14.95, ISBN: 0-935284-62-1. Paper, $9.95, ISBN: 0-935284-63-X.

Land of Enchantment; Memoirs of Marian Russell along the Santa Fe Trail, ed. by Garnet M. Brayer. 163 pages. Paper, $12.95

The Santa Fe Trail; The National Park Service 1963 Historic Sites Survey, William E. Brown. 221 pages. Cloth, $17.95, ISBN: 0-935284-64-8.

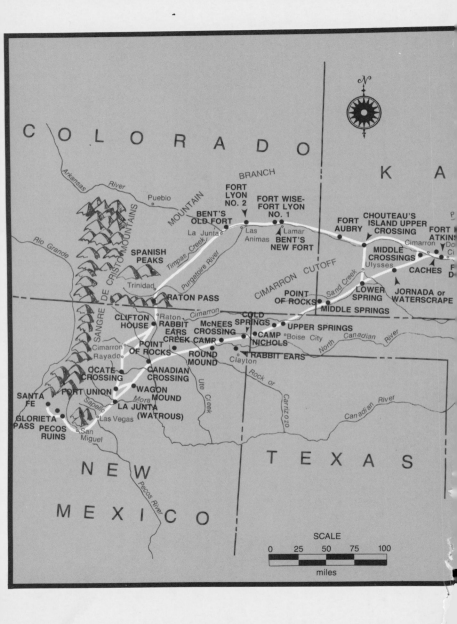